THE RECOLLECTIONS OF JOHN CULLINANE

STORIES
ALONG THE WAY

JOHN CULLINANE

By John Cullinane

Published by Omni Publishing Co.
www.omni-pub.com

Library of Congress cataloging in publication data

Cullinane, John

Stories Along the Way
The Recollections of John Cullinane

ISBN: 978-1-928758-05-1

STORIES
ALONG THE WAY

CONTENTS

CHAPTER 11 | PERSONAL 171

CHAPTER 12 | ADDENDUM 199

"A year is made up of

four seasons not

four quarters."

DEDICATION

I am pleased to dedicate this book to my wife, Diddy, and the good people who came our way as a result, including our son, John Jr., his wife Sandrine, their boys, John, Matthew, and Michael, as well as our daughter, Sue, her husband, Nat Jeppson, and the Princess in the family, Chloe.

"I have led two lives. The first was before I met Diddy Haverty, and the second was after. The second life has been much better than the first in every way."

INTRODUCTION

The idea for this book began when a good friend of Diddy's and mine, world-renowned knee surgeon Dr. Richard Scott, helped get a good friend of his to a hospital emergency room in time to possibly save his life from Covid. As a result, Dr. Scott and his wife, Mary, had to self-quarantine for 14 days. So, I wrote a story each day that I thought he might like and sent it to him to ease his boredom. He liked them so much, and he thought I had so many of them, he felt that I should put them in a book.

Diddy agreed and felt that the stories of my company, what they led to, and whom we met along the way would make for a good book and encouraged me to write it. I certainly have had the opportunity to do many interesting things with some very fascinating people. I have included a few "Early Days" stories of my youth to get started because I have led two lives. The first was before I met Diddy Haverty, and the second was after. The second life has been much better than the first in every way. Diddy was also a big help when it came to the organization and focus of this book. So was Martha Burnham, my longtime assistant.

Eventually I began sending the stories to my good friend Dr. Eric O'Brien in Dublin, who was laid up after a major operation to ease his boredom, too. He liked getting them very much and even became a very good and unanticipated editor. For example, he thought my "hole in one" story was "incredible." This meant a lot coming from a renowned Irish golfer. He, in turn, sent it to Tim Dickson, Publisher of the *Golf Quarterly*, a highly regarded British golf publication for amateurs.

The Publisher of this book, Henry Quinlan, is someone I met long ago who turned out to be a specialist in this book's space. His number one recommendation with such books is that they be anecdotal. As serendipity would have it, it was 100% anecdotal from day one.

My mother and father just married in Ireland and leaving for Boston

Brother David

Bill and Mary (Cullinane) Eidson, John Cullinane, Diddy Cullinane, and Teresa (Cullinane) Vaughan. (insert is Frank Vaughan)

Brother Jimmy

CHAPTER 1 | EARLY DAYS

GREATNESS IS WHERE YOU FIND IT

I doubt anyone passing a house at 7 Mill Street, Arlington, Massachusetts, in a blizzard on Thanksgiving Day, November 29, 1934, the day I was born, would think I was entering a great neighborhood. They probably thought the opposite, if they thought about it at all. In the house must have been my mother and father, Margaret and David Cullinane, newly arrived from Ireland, and my older siblings, Mary and Teresa, and my brother Jimmy. Not yet arrived was my younger brother David. Why it was such a great neighborhood was because just down the street was Buttrick's Dairy, which produced the greatest ice cream. People would drive from miles around to get it. Tommy O'Neill once told me his father, Tip O'Neill, would drive the family from Cambridge just for a Buttrick's ice cream cone for them. I understood why. Closest to it is the Four Seas in Centerville, JFK's favorite ice cream shop. Just up the street in the opposite direction on Mass. Avenue was Hutchinson's Candy Store, makers of the world's best chocolate fudge. Just down Mass. Avenue was the A&P bakery, makers of the world's most delicious chocolate layer cake with white frosting and coconut flakes on top. This greatness spoiled me for life at an early age because I knew what was good and what wasn't in such important matters. Then, there was Zwicker's, the world's greatest ice skate sharpeners, just down the street. One day just two doors up, Eddie Silva appeared. He would prove to be the world's greatest tackler. You wouldn't think so because he was small, skinny, and weighed only about a hundred pounds. I recruited him for our neighborhood football team that I had put together to unwisely play another neighborhood, a much bigger and meaner team, but I needed bodies. On the day of the game, we kicked off and the biggest and toughest player on the other team caught it and was running at us at full speed. Tackling him wasn't going to be fun, if we could do it at all. However, seemingly out of nowhere, Eddie darted in and hit the in-step of the runner with his little shoulder. The result was spectacular. The runner did a cartwheel before crashing to the ground. It was the greatest tackle I had ever seen. Eddie got up unscathed and kept doing it

This is a picture of the new town house located directly on the lot where my old house used to be. It's part of a very impressive town house complex. Yet, it's very similar to the original complex that was built in 1913.

the whole game. He was fearless. It was the greatest tackling performance I would ever witness, including the Patriots. Then, he disappeared as quickly as he came, as those who rented his house often did. My neighborhood was also just a short walk up the Indian Trail to Arlington High School and its football field where I would often watch the practices of the team. In 1949, when I was a sophomore, it had its greatest

"Greatness is where you find it and, in retrospect, there was a lot of greatness in my neighborhood despite appearances to the contrary."

team ever winning the Class A Championship. 20,000 people would show up to watch a game. The star running back was Donnie O'Brien, who would become a Christian Brother and was beloved by all, including opposing players. Whenever they tackled him, regardless of how hard or vicious, he would help the opposing player up and congratulate him. It was contagious because by the end of the game there was great harmony on the field as the game was played with true sportsmanship. I have never seen anything like it since. However, greatness is where you find it and, in retrospect, there was a lot of greatness in my neighborhood despite appearances to the contrary.

The Frost/O'Halloran house, the last house left in the neighborhood. It's imbedded in a large Corcoran Jennison apartment complex. Years later I became very good friends with Joe Corcoran, the developer. In his book, he said he felt sorry when he was in Park St. station coming from BC for those like me who lived in places like Arlington vs Dorchester where he lived. Ironically, I told him that I was thinking the same thing about guys like him as I was coming from Northeastern. We might have been thinking these thoughts while standing directly across the tracks from each other while waiting for a train heading in the opposite direction.

ARLINGTON FRIENDS

After the first taste of delicious lasagna at Ralph Guanci's house with Arlington friends. Just had some from Chatham Market, equally delicious.—1st Row Billy Roper. Coley Welch, Paul Welch. 2nd Row Eddie Aiken, Larry Weisbach, Ralph Guanci, Don Cahalin. 3rd Row John Cullinane, Charlie O'Neill, Bob Keating, Billy Fahey, Jack Cadagan.

ARLINGTON FRIENDS

Arlington Youth Ass'n 'Blue Jays' at Drill

Left to right - Eddie Carroll, longtime Assistant Director of Athletics at BC, John Cullinane, Jimmy Hayes, a great hitter, Jack Cadagan, successful businessman and former BC hockey Captain and Joe Cazassa, long time head of the DPW for the City of Boston.

A nicer cart of the era than mine, but the ice was the same. It melted.

THE ICEMAN COMETH

When I was about twelve, I had a newspaper route, but I had an iceman's route when I was about 8. I was the iceman for some little old ladies who would pay me ten cents to put a piece of ice in their ice boxes, good money at the time. My ice truck was an old, 1920s baby carriage that I would fill with ice and push around my route. The source of the ice was the famous Buttrick's Dairy, known for its incredibly good ice cream, located just down the street from where I lived. St. Johnsbury trucks would arrive at Buttrick's early in the morning from Vermont, unload their milk cans, and dump the ice. Their deliveries were irregular, so you could not be sure when they would happen. You just had to go every morning and hope the ice was there and you could get some of it before it was all taken by others. However, I would go all the time, not just in the morning. Others did not. This has always stayed with me. You have to work at things, and you never know when something good will happen, and it sometimes does at the most unusual time.

"I was the iceman for some little old ladies who would pay me ten cents to put a piece of ice in their ice boxes, good money at the time."

For example, once I went in the middle of a day when no one was there and found a bonanza. Big blocks of ice were everywhere. I had struck gold, and no one was around but me. The only problem was that the blocks were too big for my little eight-year-old body to lift. Worse, some of them fused with other blocks because of the sun. Here I was standing on a pile of gold, and I could not move a single piece of it, and there was no one to help. All that gold was melting away. The frustration of that moment stayed with me for years.

My paper route was long and included two distinct groups. One was relatively poor and working class. The other was quite well to do. I anticipated and was promised big Christmas tips from some of my wealthier clients. I am afraid I gave them better service in some cases than I did the poorer clients. The Christmas tips I received from the poorer group were much larger than those from the relatively rich group, despite all the promises. It was the opposite of what I expected to my great embarrassment. The poor are often more generous than the rich. This lesson has stayed with me for my whole life.

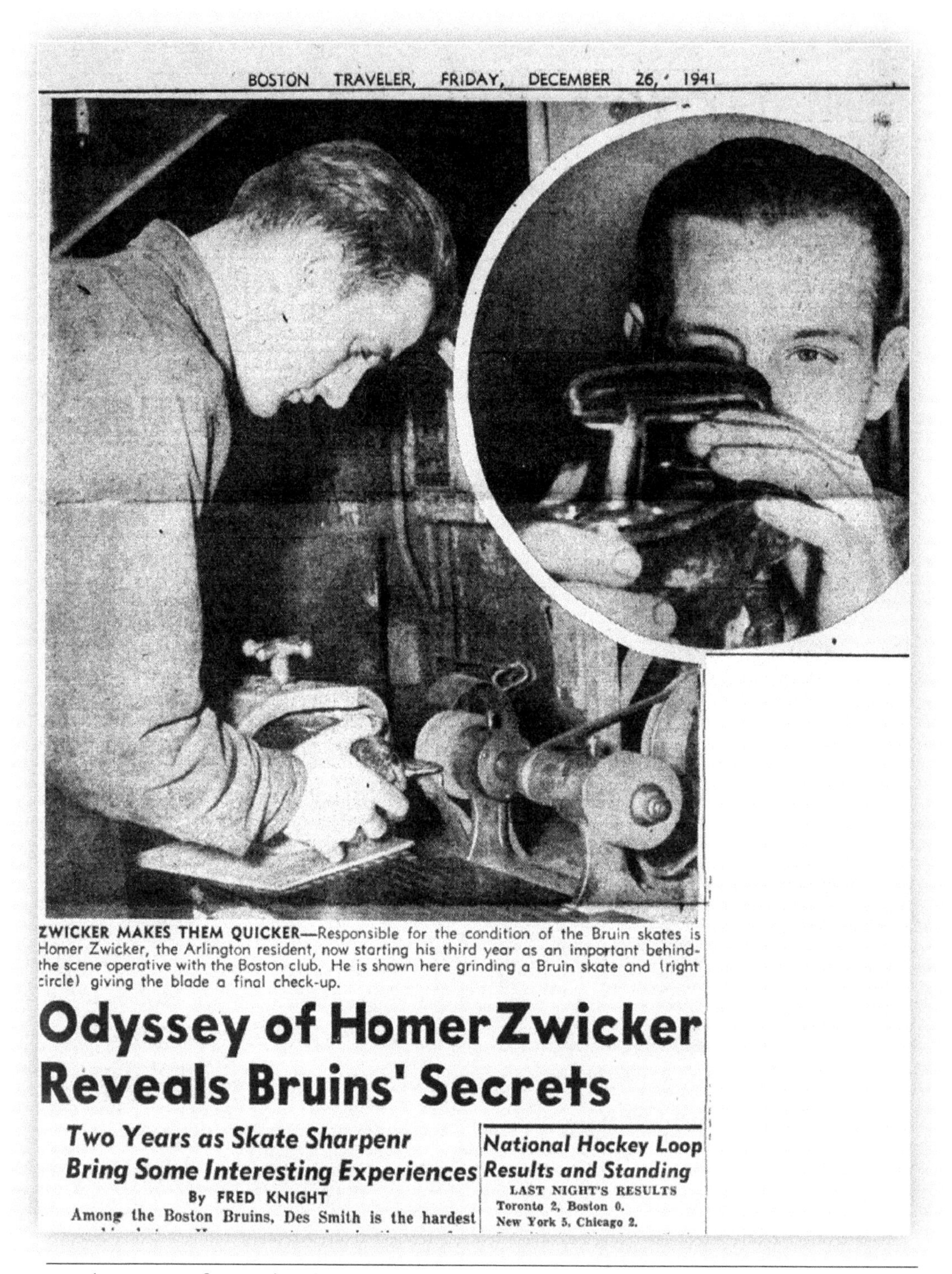

BOSTON TRAVELER, FRIDAY, DECEMBER 26, 1941

ZWICKER MAKES THEM QUICKER—Responsible for the condition of the Bruin skates is Homer Zwicker, the Arlington resident, now starting his third year as an important behind-the scene operative with the Boston club. He is shown here grinding a Bruin skate and (right circle) giving the blade a final check-up.

Odyssey of Homer Zwicker Reveals Bruins' Secrets

Two Years as Skate Sharpenr Bring Some Interesting Experiences

By FRED KNIGHT

Among the Boston Bruins, Des Smith is the hardest

National Hockey Loop Results and Standing

LAST NIGHT'S RESULTS

Toronto 2, Boston 0.

New York 5, Chicago 2.

Article courtesy of Ira Goding (see page 16), given to me when he was 100.
Note the date on the newspaper.

ZWICKERS

Zwickers' reputation was so powerful that people would wait all day to get their skates sharpened. Almost all local high school and college teams had their skates sharpened at Zwickers. So did the Boston Bruins. You might not win the big game if Zwickers had not sharpened your skates.

The best part of my job at Zwickers was the Bruins. Mr. Zwicker, the father, and Homer, the son, who was big and tall and looked like John Wayne, would take me to the Bruins games when they did the Bruins' skates. First, we would have a wonderful meal of real Nantucket scallops at the Union Oyster House. It's one of those meals that looks and tastes just as good today as I remember it. During the hockey game, Homer would stand behind the Bruins bench in case a player's skate needed work. This left two excellent seats for Mr. Zwicker and me. I saw every Bruins game for

"I would handle the skates of such greats as Rocket Richard, Gordie Howe, Jean Beliveau."

two years. Often, I would have to go into the Bruins locker room between periods to bring a newly sharpened skate. Sometimes we would have to stay afterward and sharpen the visitor teams' skates if they were all going on the road. I would handle the skates of such greats as Rocket Richard, Gordie Howe, Jean Beliveau, etc. Most hockey players were small at the time, maybe, 5 feet 7 inches. Beliveau was considered huge at 6 feet 3 inches.

Sometimes I would drive Zwicker's van right into the Boston Garden with the skates and put them in the dressing room since I had the key. I would take the opportunity to try on some of the equipment. Once I saw the great Bruins Captain, Milt Schmidt, coming toward me and said, "Hello, Mr. Schmidt." He responded, "Call me Milt." I was impressed. I saw him a couple of times a few years ago in a Needham barber shop. He was ninety-eight and still a formidable presence. One night, I was in the dressing room wearing a new winter jacket when Fleming Mackell, a big star, said, "Hey kid. Come here. Where did you get the jacket?" I told him I had just bought it in Filene's Basement. He was wearing a similar one-two weeks later but, frankly, I did not think it was as nice as mine. All heady stuff for a 16-year-old. Zwickers still exists in Bedford, Massachusetts, run by Wayne Zwicker, Homer's son.

The Diamond T tractor I drove at age 17 was much bigger than this one. It also had ten forward speeds and two reverse.

THEY DRIVE BY NIGHT

JK McKeown was a furniture moving company just up the street from my house. I was a "working man" there, from time to time, starting when I was 17. Every so often, we would go "on the road." This meant leaving at midnight. It was very exciting since I had never been anywhere before. As far as the eye could see, the night was full of trucks moving in both directions. Once, the driver was so tired that he let me drive our huge Diamond T trailer truck up the New Jersey Turnpike while he slept in the back bunk. The speedometer was broken so I had no idea how fast I was going but we made it in record time. It had ten forward speeds and two reverse, which impresses my grandsons.

The Jersey Turnpike had a Service Area in East Brunswick named after Joyce Kilmer. He was the author of the first poem I can remember, "Trees." It was taught to every student in parochial school. "I think that I shall never see a poem lovely as a tree." When I mentioned it to Diddy, she could recite the whole poem. Odd that they would name a stop on the Jersey Pike after him. There were no trees that I can remember. They were all cut down.

"Once, the driver was so tired that he let me drive our huge Diamond T trailer truck up the New Jersey Turnpike while he slept in the back bunk."

On one of these trips, I witnessed a Black man we picked up to help unload the truck on one stop get cheated. He was paid half of what he should have been, but he could not do anything about it. He was a good worker and very intelligent, too. He just looked at the pittance in such a way that you knew what he was thinking. This had a lasting impact on me. It was not fair.

I had several such jobs before I finally joined the management class up from the working class. Before I attended my first corporate management meeting, I was in the hotel pool on a sweltering day at a first-class hotel. A fellow manager who was also in the pool spent most of the time complaining about how difficult our jobs were. I thought, "This is difficult?"

This is not Jasper, but close because he has Jasper's look about him.

JASPER

Jasper was the name of the only dog I ever had. He was a small black, yellow and white Beagle/Dachshund mongrel. I did not ask for him; I was just given him one day. He was not an impressive-looking dog at all. He even had a bit of a mean streak and would bite people in the neighborhood. I would be put in an awkward position of having to defend him, even though I knew he was probably guilty. Worse, I am not sure he even liked me very much. However, it was clear that he liked my brother-in-law, Frank Vaughan, more. Jasper liked the attention and the rough-house way Frank played with him, even holding him up by his hind legs.

One summer, I watched a twilight baseball game at the Arlington High School field with Jasper lying contentedly beside me on the grass. We were located down the first baseline toward the outfield. It was the last inning, and one team had the bases loaded with two outs. The batter hit a hard line drive just inside the first

"Jasper, in a remarkable demonstration of agility and reflexes that I had never seen before, leaped into the air and caught the ball cleanly in his teeth."

base line, fair. It hit the ground just before us and bounced high into the air. In a remarkable demonstration of agility and reflexes that I had never seen before, Jasper leaped into the air and caught the ball cleanly in his teeth. It was a very impressive feat. Unfortunately, it did not end there. Jasper took off at high speed down the line and out the gate disappearing in the distance with the ball firmly in his mouth. The baseball players were furious at this development and demanded to know if it was my dog or not. I am afraid that I denied knowing him.

Later that night, Jasper appeared back at home with a smile, but minus the ball. I sensed that he finally felt pretty good about himself, that he felt he had done something really big. He had.

Ira Goding

IRA GODING

I first met Ira Goding when he returned from WWII after spending four years fighting across Europe in the Army. He had volunteered after Pearl Harbor even though he had just spent six years as an enlisted man in the 1930s at Schofield Barracks in Hawaii, the site of the book and movie, "From Here to Eternity." He even played baseball with Joe DiMaggio there.

Ira ran the Boston & Maine railroad gates that crossed Mill Street not far from where I lived. He would play baseball with us between his morning and evening shifts when the trains ran. He even took me to about 20 Red Sox games during the 1946 pennant year. Coming out of the walkway under the Fenway Park stands for the first time and seeing that great green park was an incredible experience. Everybody feels the same way. However, I was stunned that Rudy York was bald when he took off his hat when they played the National Anthem. I thought that they were all just young men. Funny, the things you remember.

"Congresswoman Clark arranged to fly an American flag in his honor at the Capitol Building."

Ira would eventually disappear, though. I always wondered what happened to him, so years later I tried googling him. Amazingly, I found an Ira Goding living in St. Petersburg, Florida, and with ties to Lexington, Massachusetts. He was 99 years old, the right age. I sent him a letter, and it was he. Eventually, we met when he came north, and I even went to his 100th birthday celebration. Incidentally, CVS has birthday cards for 100-year-olds. The Red Sox even invited him to throw out the first ball, but he declined even though he was still in great shape, walking three miles a day. Ira died at age 107. I asked my friends in Washington, D.C., if there was any way they could recognize Ira for all he did for our country. They said yes, and Congresswoman Clark arranged to fly an American flag in his honor at the Capitol Building. Afterward, they sent it to his family, who were most appreciative. Also, it seems very timely. He fought for our Democracy.

Northeastern University

Arthur D. Little, Inc., headquarters in Cambridge, Massachusetts

OPPORTUNITY

I was a classic screwup in high school, looking for attention in the wrong ways. I barely graduated. Thanks to Miss Fitzpatrick, my guidance counselor, and my sisters' exemplary records, I did. This was followed by various low-level jobs, including one in marine plumbing in East Boston. I hated it, and I could sense the world was passing me by. Many of the guys I fooled around with in high school did their homework and were now off at college. I was being left behind. I did one smart thing, though. I tried to get the best score on an IQ test the school had us take. Miss Fitzpatrick helped me get into Northeastern University. She did not have to help me, but she did.

"Northeastern would open the all-important door of opportunity for me at Arthur D. Little, Inc., via its Co-op program. ADL was a world-renowned industrial research firm of the time."

Northeastern would open the all-important door of opportunity for me at Arthur D. Little, Inc., via its Co-op program. ADL was a world-renowned industrial research firm of the time. The key that opened all the other doors was when it installed one of the first commercially available computers next to my office.

Northeastern also had an incredibly diverse student body, which was valuable for someone who had grown up, as I had, in a traditional Irish Catholic family and schools. There were students with all kinds of backgrounds that I had never had any contact with before. It was a mind-opening experience.

We had to attend school for five years, though. The first year was tough because it went thirty-five straight weeks without any time off. However, I lived at home, commuted to school, got a degree, made enough money from my Co-op job to pay for tuition, got job experience, and had lots of job offers when I graduated. I also had no debt, and neither did my parents. What's wrong with that educational model?

Diddy's mother Agnes MacIsaac

Diddy's father Martin F. Haverty

Diddy's brother Charlie, and a Captain in the Marine Corps

Diddy, Mrs. Haverty, sisters Claire and Rose

Diddy at the Nobles rink

ACROSS A CROWDED ROOM

I was in Falmouth on Cape Cod as a student during the waning hours of Labor Day when this girl across a crowded room caught my eye with her beautiful smile. She was talking to some guy, but he left. I waited for him to return, but he didn't. So, I went over and said hello, and she said hello back. Simple, but I had never done anything like that before. I never let her go.

Her name was Diddy Haverty, the most beautiful, nicest, and smartest girl that I had ever met, and quite mysterious, too. How was it she spoke so well? Even Senator Ed Markey, an astute observer, once asked her, "Who are you?" She was brought up in Dorchester and lived in Roslindale, but she had no Boston accent. Her mother was a Scot from Nova Scotia, and her family could all speak well and with no Canadian accents. Her father's side was from South Boston, and he spoke and wrote beautifully. I guess it is all in the genes.

She was a second-grade school teacher when I met her, having finished first in the City of Boston's teacher exam. She could also paint and even sold one of a boat for $50 to the owner. She also had a car that she bought for $50 that she would lend me to drive home from Roslindale to Arlington after dates. It made for some interesting experiences getting home, but much better than taking the T.

Diddy at the beach in Nantasket

Claire Eldracher, Diddy's sister, me, Diddy and Frank Vaughan at our wedding

CHAPTER 2 | FAMILY

THE CULLINANES

The newlyweds, Mr. and Mrs. John Cullinane

Sandrine and John Jr. married in Cambridge, Massachusetts

John Jr. already showing hitting prowess with my mother's cane.

JOHN JR. & SANDRINE CULLINANE FAMILY

Diddy produced two outstanding children, John, Jr., and Sue. At two years old, John Jr., already so loved baseball that he dragged a bat around with him. One day I threw a plastic ball to him on the front lawn to see if he could hit it. I had to duck; he hit it back so hard. A guy driving by saw it and yelled, "Sign him up!" He was blessed with excellent eye/hand coordination, thanks to his mother.

When he was about eight years old, we were at Fenway Park sitting down the left-field line when a batter hit a curving line drive down the left-field line. Everyone ducked, but when we looked up, the ball was in John's glove. Many people brought transistor radios to the game in those days, and you could hear Ned Martin, the Red Sox broadcaster, saying all over the park, "What a great catch a kid just made!" A nearby drunk got up and shouted at me, "What is his name? I want to vote for him for the All-Star team!" Voting was taking place that day. On the way home, I asked John, "What will you do if you make the All-Star team? Are you going to play?" John thought seriously about it for a long time, as he was wont to do, and then answered, "Yes."

John is a graduate of Harvard College and Harvard Business School and has a very successful private equity company. He has three sons, John, Matthew, and Michael, thanks to his wife Sandrine, from Paris. Now, he is helping a Harvard classmate of his, Father Paul O'Brien, raise money to build a new school at St. Patrick's in Lawrence, Massachusetts.

Matthew, Michael and John skating at Fenway Park

Sue and Nat Jeppson married in Chatham, Massachusetts

SUE & NAT JEPPSON FAMILY

Sue is a Primary Care Physician at Mass General Hospital working at a clinic in Chelsea, Massachusetts, an epicenter of the Covid disease. Sue graduated from Harvard College and Columbia Physicians and Surgeons in New York. She was also Chief Resident at New York Presbyterian Hospital.

Sue has always had a flair for things. For example, while she was attending medical school in New York City she was invited to see a Knick's game at Madison Square Garden. She was stopped on the way in and asked if she wanted to shoot baskets during the half as part of a contest. Naturally, she agreed without hesitation, I am sure, and was introduced to the 17,000 in attendance. She swished the first basket and won $100 with the crowd cheering her on and her name going around the arena on the displays. Then, she moved back to shoot again. This time she would win a jeep if she sank a shot. She did not, but the crowd was still cheering her on. This was her five-minute basketball career. She also Co-Captained Harvard in hockey. Sue is married to Nat Jeppson, President of a money management firm. He comes from a family with a long Worcester tradition, including the founding of Norton Abrasives. His Mother, Gabriella De Ferrari, is a noted author from Peru. They have a daughter, Chloe, who is the Princess of the family and loves hockey and lacrosse.

Chloe

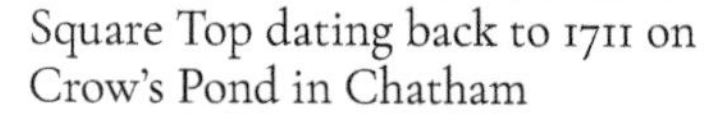

Square Top dating back to 1711 on Crow's Pond in Chatham

Family picture of my mother's birthday at Square Top in Chatham

Sue performing in the McMullen Family Dance Act at The Chatham Bars Inn

Walking Sue down the aisle

Friends Peter Lacaillade, Copey Coppedge and Owen Larkin singing with enthusiasm at our annual summer party. Behind them is Senator Paul Tsongas

John as a member of Westwood Legion All-Star Team

CHATHAM

When my company went public, we made enough money to buy a property in Chatham, Massachusetts. Diddy found a place called "Square Top" that she liked very much. It was a big property owned by General Lucius Clay, of Berlin Airlift fame. It was on Crow's Pond with an outlet to the sea and close by Eastward Ho! Golf Club.

I learned how to do all those things I never did growing up, such as swimming, sailing, boating, water skiing, saltwater fishing, shell fishing, etc. I learned that if there is an oil slick around a boat engine, it might be leaking oil regardless of what the mechanic says. I took Diddy out for the first run on my new (used) boat toward sunset, and the engine froze for lack of oil. The sun was going down, the tide was going out through Bassing Harbor, and the wind was blowing hard, and we were moving with it. We had a very dicey time trying to paddle the boat to shore. When we landed, we knocked on the door of the first house we came to, and the woman who answered seemed very happy to see us. She even gave us a tour of her interesting home filled with antiques. When the tour was over, I thumbed a ride for us around Crow's Pond to home. As we came through the front door and out the back door, we saw John and Sue down on the dock looking out, very worried about us, a role model reversal. Everyone has been suspicious of my boating skills ever since.

On a happier note, I encountered some local kids who said they needed players for their Chatham baseball team. I called the coach, Noel Kinski, about John, Jr., joining the team. He asked me if John could pitch and play first base. I said that is what he does, and he was an all-star in Westwood, so it was a perfect fit. With John pitching, Chatham won the game, 1-0, to win the championship for the first time in its history, even though the opposing pitcher pitched a no-hitter. As a father, it's great to witness your son's sports highlights. It was also gratifying to know he had a great coach like Kinski.

Our daughter, Sue, would become part of the McMullen Family's Saturday Night Dance Act at The Chatham Bars Inn, which they owned. Thus, we would go every Saturday night to see our eleven-year-old daughter in "show business." She also learned how to do all the dances.

Diddy put on great summer parties at Square Top with sing-alongs and would invite all the neighbors, Tip O'Neill, and many others. Across the pond was the Avalon Camp for Girls. They would sail their little boats up to our lawn when we had a party and sing their songs at night. It was all idyllic.

Bobby Orr and Mrs. Haverty, the two Canadians

MRS. HAVERTY

Mrs. Haverty, Diddy's mother, was a Scotswoman from Sydney, Nova Scotia. Her first job in Boston was as a 17-year-old nurse in training at Carney Hospital, South Boston, during the deadly 1917 Spanish Flu Pandemic, with young soldiers dying all around her. Eventually she would meet her husband, Martin "Frank" Haverty, at a dance in South Boston.

Mrs. Haverty loved watching sports on television, particularly hockey games with Bobby Orr and the Boston Bruins. Mrs. Haverty's brother, Duke MacIsaac, was a renowned goalie in Nova Scotia and the first player elected to the Nova Scotia Hockey Hall of Fame. He also had offers from the Toronto Maple Leafs, but chose to go to Dalhousie University, where he was Captain of the hockey team that would play Harvard in 1920.

"Mrs. Haverty loved watching sports on television, particularly hockey games with Bobby Orr and the Boston Bruins."

We hosted an annual Christmas party at our home in Dedham and invited all the neighbors and their guests. One of them was a Mr. Higgins. In an incredible coincidence, we learned that he was also a goalie and Captain of the 1920 Harvard hockey team that played Duke MacIsaac's team. Harvard beat Dalhousie, much to Duke's chagrin.

But, back to Mrs. Haverty. When Bobby Orr agreed to join my company's Board of Directors, I said I would only ask him to do one favor for me: to visit Mrs. Haverty, whose house was close to our offices. So, it was all arranged without Mrs. Haverty's knowledge. As Bobby and I pulled up in front of her house in separate cars, she looked out the window, saw us, and said to Diddy, "Someone is getting out of a car with Jack." Then she recognized him and exclaimed, "It's Bobby Orr!" She greeted him at the door and gave him a big hug as he did her. After all, they were fellow Canadians. Great moments in sports and the beginning of a warm relationship.

My mother and Mrs. Haverty at a User Week. They took to the good life like they were born to the purple.

Art Buchwald and the Belles are having a good time. He liked it too.

Dancing with Diddy's mother.

THE BELLES OF THE BALL

When my company was having its first User Group meeting in Orlando, Florida, I asked Diddy to attend, but it was not something she was keen on doing. She suggested I take my mother. This was not practical, but I thought it could work if Diddy's mother would accompany her. So, this began a wonderful series of events for them when they were in their eighties. I would give them my "comped" Presidential Suite, show them how to use room service, and they were on their way. At the Doral Hotel, they gave them a golf cart, and they could drive anywhere they wanted.

On Wednesday evenings during the User Group event, they would attend the big gala with humorists such as Art Buchwald, a dance band, etc. They would even be asked to dance by some of our older customers. It was miraculous to watch the age just disappear from their faces. They became girls again, the Belles of the Ball. They would talk about their experiences for a year until the next User Group meeting, thinking it would never be as good as the last one. Yet, it would turn out to be better.

"It was miraculous to watch the age just disappear from their faces. They became girls again, the Belles of the Ball."

In Las Vegas, my wife's mother even got to play Blackjack, which she loved. My mother played along, watching her every move, trying to copy it. She had never played Blackjack before or even been in a casino. Before long, a crowd gathered around them as my wife's mother was very personable and witty. One of my clients owned casinos in Las Vegas, so I knew how they worked, how some people would try to beat the house, how they controlled slot machines, etc. For example, they blew oxygen through the air conditioning system at 4:00 am to keep people awake and gambling. I also knew there were employees above the ceiling looking down for possible scams. I am sure they were wondering what these not so little old ladies down there were up to. They had not seen this one before. A competitor said that I was even using my mother to sell software.

David and Margaret Fitzgerald Cullinane Hall Dedication—(l-r) John Cullinane, Diddy Cullinane, Margaret Cullinane, Bernard Cardinal Law, Northeastern President Ken Ryder, and Senator Edward Kennedy.

CULLINANE HALL

Roy Toebes, a dynamo fundraiser for Northeastern University, called me one day and said Northeastern wanted to name a building after me that would house the College of Computer Science. It was one of Northeastern's oldest buildings but completely done over. I said, "That's nice but don't name it for me, name it after my parents; David and Margaret Cullinane."

At the time, my uncle and family favorite, Willie Fitzgerald, recently had a stroke. He had always followed my company closely. I visited him, and all he could say was, "No." I told him that we were having the building dedication and would add the Fitzgerald name on the building as follows, "The David and Margaret Fitzgerald Cullinane Hall." He smiled. He died that night.

"Cullinane Hall still exists at Northeastern University, with the cartouche that Diddy designed still hanging outside the building."

At the building dedication event, I handed the microphone to my mother to say a few words. She had never spoken into a microphone before, but she handled it so well that she was the star of the event with her soft Irish accent. Never follow your mother on stage.

Cullinane Hall still exists at Northeastern University, with the cartouche that Diddy designed still hanging outside the building. The College of Computer Science has since moved to a beautiful new building and received a $60 million donation. Cullinane Hall is probably one of the oldest and least impressive buildings on the campus these days, but it doesn't bother me. I like it. It has character and history and, besides, it served its purpose.

Cullinane Hall and cartouche designed by Diddy

Mrs. Margaret Fitzgerald Cullinane of Harvard Chambermaids

HARVARD

Our grandson, Matthew, is currently at Harvard. However, my mother went to Harvard, too, in her own way. This is what I tell Matthew. She took the bus every day to Harvard Square, with good friend Mrs. Ellen Keohane, to work at Radcliffe as a chambermaid. However, my mother was very intelligent, social, and very well-read. She liked the students very much, and they liked her. They used to talk often and were very interested in her background as an immigrant, her soft Irish accent, where she came from, how she survived, etc. They learned a lot from each other.

When my son, John Jr., graduated, there was a long list of interviews of seniors in *The Harvard Gazette* about what they learned at Harvard. Each said the same thing.

"My mother was certainly a positive contributor to and beneficiary of the Harvard scene in her years there. She earned her virtual degree."

The people they met there and what they learned from them was most important. Using these criteria, my mother was certainly a positive contributor to and beneficiary of the Harvard scene in her years there. She earned her virtual degree.

My wife and I were Co-Chairs of the Harvard Parents Fund for three years. The Harvard Parents Fund is comprised of parents and grandparents of students of Harvard who did not go to Harvard. It was a very good group to Chair since they were all very delighted to have their children or grandchildren at Harvard. There were no complaints. One evening after being at a Parents Fund event and listening to a Nobel Laureate in Chemistry, I went to the bar. The only other person there before me was the famed actor Theodore Bikel. Neither of us knew quite what to say to break the ice, but he spoke first and said, "We must have done something right." That seemed to say it all.

The view from our room at The Savoy Hotel in London

CELTIC STUDIES

Diddy and I were invited to a black-tie dinner at the President's House at Harvard on behalf of the Friends of Harvard's Celtic Studies Program. Sitting next to me was Seamus Heaney, world-renowned Irish poet, Nobel Laureate and Visiting Professor in Celtic Studies. I first heard of him when my son, John Jr., took his course at Harvard.

After the dinner, Professor Patrick Ford, Head of the Celtic Studies Program, spoke. He expressed his desire to raise a certain amount of money for the program. It was a very modest amount by Harvard's standards. With two Harvard graduates, a son and a daughter, we were long overdue to do something for Harvard. So, after Professor Ford finished speaking, I went up to him and asked if he would accept a donation even if it was more than he asked.

Harvard made much of the donation. They had a cocktail party, and The Friends presented Diddy and me with a very nice, inscribed dish. There was even an extensive article in *The Harvard Gazette* about the event. At the presentation, I said, "Never in the history of Harvard has anyone given so little and received so much recognition." Jack Reardon, Assistant Director of Development at Harvard at the time, smiled. He knew that we had been treated very well.

Associate Vice President for University Relations John P. "Jack" Reardon Jr., donor Diddy Cullinane, department chair Patrick K. Ford, donor John Cullinane, British Consul General James Poston, and Irish Consul General Conor O'Riordan at the announcement of the Cullinane's gift to the Department of Celtic Languages and Literatures.

With Mark Volpe at Wequassett Inn for an event we hosted for the BSO on Cape Cod.

Jim O'Brien, Niki Tsongas, Diddy, Kathryn and John Hamill at Wequassett BSO event.

THE BOSTON SYMPHONY ORCHESTRA (BSO)

The BSO is like a big family we were lucky to be part of. It began when Diddy was recruited by Dr. Nick Zervas for the Board of Overseers, became Chair, and then Chair of the Nominating Committee of the Board of Trustees. She is now a Life Trustee. Mark Volpe was the Director and then President. I do not know how he kept track of it because there is an Orchestra, Tanglewood, and the POPs. On top of that, there are unions, artists, tours, maestros, traveling, and much more, such as raising money.

To help with that, Diddy and I co-hosted two Opening Nights for the BSO, including one in 2009 when the market was crashing. Yet, we raised just more than $1 million with an imaginative use of the BSO's trusted website, which had millions of visitors a year. This was twice the amount of money that was raised the year before. After Diddy mentioned that we were close to raising $1 million, Peter Lacaillade volunteered to come up with the last $3,500 to push us over the $1 million mark at the event.

At dinner afterward, I introduced Diddy by saying:

"When my company was flying high, I used to be introduced at these events as --

Mr. John Cullinane

Then it became Mr. and Mrs. John Cullinane

Then it became John and Diddy Cullinane

Then it became Diddy and John Cullinane

Diddy interrupted with, "Not true!" and everyone laughed. But I was kicking myself for not responding that recently I had been sitting with my four-year-old grandson, Michael, the "Philosopher" in the family. He was staring at me intently for some time, then he said, "What's your name again?" I am sure it would have broken up the audience as it did me. Afterward, whenever I saw him, I would always ask him, "What's my name again?" One day when he was about six, he muttered, "I'm not answering that question anymore."

John Friar, Dan Gregory, Tony De Ritis

4 Phases of Entrepreneurship and How to Cope With Them

John Cullinane formed the first successful software products company in the computer industry at a time when industry gurus said that it couldn't be done, others had tried and failed, and so would he. However, his company's IPO succeeded so dramatically that it proved to Wall Street, and the computer industry, that a great deal of money could be made from treating software as a product. Many software companies followed and an industry was born.

However, like any entrepreneur, he had to manage his company through the four phases of any new venture which always begins

Featured Book

The Entrepreneur's Survival Guide – 101 Tips for Managing in Good Times & Bad
Every entrepreneur, executive and manager hopes for quick, consistent growth, but not many are ready for it when it happens. John Cullinane, one of the pioneers of the computer software industry, presents crucial lessons he learned from his company's founding. more »

Cullinane Active Archive

TONY DE RITIS

At a Trustees, Overseers, and spouses meeting of the Boston Symphony Orchestra, Mark Volpe presented a new e-learning system called Online Conservatory for understanding the music and its composers at BSO concerts. It was very impressive and, when he said it was created with Northeastern University, I was curious. I did not know Northeastern had a music program. So, I tracked down the person who created it, Tony De Ritis, who would prove to be a very bright, imaginative, and entrepreneurial individual. This contact would lead to a meeting between Tony and Dan Gregory, Jr., someone very knowledgeable in venture capital and an active entrepreneur in the digital media industry. Dan, as a result, would become interested in academia and would join Northeastern in a teaching role. Eventually, he would become a significant force in the already impressive entrepreneurship program under Professors Marc Meyer, John Friar, and others. The result was that Northeastern has the most comprehensive entrepreneurship program in academia anywhere. I think President Aoun, early on, bought into all this entrepreneurship to help him realize the great potential of the Northeastern educational model as he transformed the school into the powerhouse it has become.

Good things always seemed to come out of interactions with Tony. For example, when we were last moving, I wondered what I would do with all the corporate memorabilia. Could it be used to benefit other potential entrepreneurs and academicians? Tony suggested we meet with Dan Cohen, the new Dean of the Northeastern Library. Out of this meeting came the idea for an "active" archive.

The site enabled my grandchildren to see what their grandfather did and view other family videos such as the Cullinane Hall Dedication, etc.

Otherwise, all this material, particularly these one-of-a-kind videos, would be buried in boxes and lost. It was all remarkably easy to do. I had the videos digitized at "Play it Again." My ISP supplier, Margaret Aranyosi of Bold Everything Interactive, loaded them on YouTube. I wrote the narrative for the archive, including selecting the pictures. Martha Burnham, my long-time assistant, and non-technician, learned how to use WordPress to create the site using this input. Margaret put it all on her ISP, and we were in business.

"VIP Chorus members such as Bill Bulger, Mike Dukakis, and many others were paying strict attention to Diddy as she rehearsed them."

Tip O'Neill conducting, and members of the VIP Chorus singing with gusto.

TIP O'NEILL EVENT

There is nothing Diddy likes better than producing events such as the Boston Public Library Galas or honoring Tip O'Neill at Symphony Hall on behalf of Catholic Charities. She even produced great events for our children and their classmates when they were in grammar school.

I was backstage when she rehearsed the VIP Chorus, which she put together for the Tip O'Neill event. The VIP Chorus would be singing the words she wrote, celebrating Tip to Irish music that the POPs knew. I watched as VIP Chorus members such as Bill Bulger, Mike Dukakis, and many others were paying strict attention to Diddy as she rehearsed them. It made me smile because all these very powerful people looked like they were all back in the second grade again, and she was their teacher, as she once was. There is no one more authoritative, in my opinion, than a second-grade schoolteacher. Incidentally, Mike Dukakis turned out to have a great voice. It came as a great surprise to everyone.

I sat up in the first balcony with Tip, and his wife, Millie. He was not going to participate because he was not feeling well. However, he could not just sit up there while all those others were having a great time on stage in his honor. So, he got up and went down the stairs and conducted the orchestra and the chorus. And then he sang, "I'll Be With You in Apple Blossom Time" to Millie as she looked down from the balcony. Tip brought the house down.

V.I.P. CHORUS

Anthony Athanas
Anthony's Pier 4 Restaurant
Honorable Edward P. Boland
Honorable William M. Bulger
President of the Senate
Commonwealth of Massachusetts
John T. Campbell
WPLM-FM
Julia Child
Billy Chin
Donald J. Chiofaro
The Chiofaro Company
Karen A. Clark
USTrust Company
James F. Cleary
PaineWebber, Inc.
William F. Connell
Connell Limited Partnership
S. James Coppersmith
WCVB-TV5
Joseph E. Corcoran
Corcoran Jennison Companies
David W. Cowens
The Sports Museum
Honorable Robert Q. Crane
Treasurer
Commonwealth of Massachusetts
Chet Curtis
WCVB-TV5
Honorable Michael S. Dukakis
Governor
Commonwealth of Massachusetts
Robert P. Fitzgerald
Corroon & Black of Massachusetts, Inc.
Thomas J. Flatley
The Flatley Company
John P. Hamill
The Shawmut Bank N.A.
Jack Hynes
WLVI-TV56
Natalie Jacobson
WCVB-TV5
Dean Hubert E. Jones
Boston University School of Social Work
Honorable George Keverian
Speaker
Massachusetts House of Representatives
Paul G. Kirk, Jr., Esq.
Sullivan & Worcester
Judy Kurland
Commissioner
Department of Health & Hospitals
Will McDonough
The Boston Globe/CBS-TV
J. Donald Monan, S.J.
President, Boston College
Joe Morgan
The Boston Red Sox
Honorable David S. Nelson
U.S. District Judge
Peter F. O'Connell
Kirk O'Donnell
Center for National Policy
Eileen Prose
WCVB-TV5 "Good Day!"
Patrick J. Purcell
The Boston Herald
Kenneth G. Ryder
Chancellor
Northeastern University
Kate Sullivan
WNEV-TV7
William H. Sullivan, Jr.
New England Patriots
Stephen J. Sweeney
Boston Edison Company
William O. Taylor
The Boston Globe
Senator Paul E. Tsongas
Foley, Hoag & Eliot
Jack Williams
WBZ-TV4
Robert G. Woolf
Bob Woolf Associates, Inc.

I only regret that I did not join the Chorus when I had the chance and watch Tip conduct both the orchestra and the Chorus. One good thing was that since I had just sold my company, I had invited all employees, and their spouses, to the event plus anyone else that had any remote connection to the company as a way of saying thanks. It also meant for a big crowd in the hall. They all loved it.

Cullinet

CULLINET SOFTWARE, INC.

Authorised	Issued, and reserved for issue, as of 31st October, 1984*
80,000,000	**20,525,604**

Common Stock of U.S. $.10 par value

*Including 1,509,604 shares held in Treasury.

Cullinet Software, Inc., headquartered in Westwood, Massachusetts, is the world's leading independent software company. Cullinet develops and markets database management software for building systems and controlling data resources, and integrated applications software for manufacturing, finance, human resources and banking. The Company also provides integrated software for personal computers and mainframe software that links users of personal computers to corporate information. In 1984, the Company had net revenue of U.S.$120,036,000 and net income of U.S.$16,494,000.

The Council of The Stock Exchange has admitted to the Official List all the 20,525,604 shares of Common Stock of Cullinet Software, Inc., including 1,509,604 shares held in Treasury.

Particulars relating to Cullinet are available in the Extel Statistical Service and copies of such particulars, together with copies of the latest audited financial statements, may be obtained during usual business hours on any weekday (Saturdays and public holidays excepted) up to and including 21st January, 1985 from:

Goldman Sachs International Corp.,
162 Queen Victoria Street,
London EC4V 4DB

Morgan Grenfell & Co. Limited,
23 Great Winchester Street,
London EC2P 2AX

Phillips & Drew,
120 Moorgate,
London EC2M 6XP

31st December, 1984

Cullinet stock

CHAPTER 3 | COMPANY

COMPANY

I ran into a former associate at Logan Airport, Gil Curtis, who said that if I ever wanted to do something on my own, to let him know. He would be interested in doing it with me. This got me thinking about forming a company because I had very high regard for Gil. We had been successful at a previous company developing software systems as a team. Selling them as a product was the idea for a company I had for some time. Eventually, I came home from work one day and told Diddy, "I'm thinking about forming my own company." She said, "Go ahead and do it. If it does not work out, I can always get a job teaching." This was the key encouragement I needed. It took all the pressure off.

What pushed me over the line to start a company was the meeting I just had with the President of the computer consulting company I worked for. He was in town to present me with an Outstanding Performance Award for opening the highly successful Boston office. The award turned out to be such a ridiculously small amount, $500, payable over three years, with no vested rights. My immediate reaction as he told me this was, "I'm going to form that company I have been thinking about."

The idea for a company specializing in software as a product came to me when I was working as VP of Marketing at a traditional computer consulting and programming firm of the time. Gil Curtis and Anna Marie Thron had designed and programmed a generalized payroll system for three banks in a row that I had sold. In each case, despite doubling the price, we overran the contract. We finished the third payroll system when another bank called looking for a similar payroll system. They even had the same computer system. I thought, why don't we sell them the system we just finished versus creating another custom version? Why re-invent the wheel? Amazingly, this was a pretty novel thought at the time. We did, and it was an eye-opening experience. We had them up and running the system in two weeks, they were thrilled, paid the invoice right away, and it was very profitable. What is wrong with that?

Gil and Anna Marie would join the company and develop its first successful products.

Ted Rosen, the Indestructible Man

INVESTMENT BANKERS

George White would have a significant impact on my career. First, he hired me as a sales trainee at CEIR. Then he gave me my first promotion, which led to other good things. When I started looking to raise money for my company, Boston did not look too promising. So, I sought out George, who was willing to help, and he introduced me to Sol Manber. Sol liked to invest in startups and introduced me to his friend Ted Rosen at Burnham & Co., on Wall Street. Incidently, Ted Rosen was once featured in a *Ripley's Believe It or Not!* as an "Indestructible Man" in WWII. A company Sol was involved in, Alphanumeric, Inc., had gone public at $6 a share and was now selling at $609, so anything Sol was investing in was good enough for them. My actual investment bankers were Howard Goldberg and John Matkovich. Howard had some problems with his mother, so you could never call him Howie, which she called him. Howard dressed like he was out of "The Godfather," grey fedora hat, a long black coat, and a big cigar. John Matkovich was a former Christian brother who used expressions like "Jesus, Mary, and Joseph" and "God Willing," etc. It was like I was listening to my Irish Catholic mother, only on Wall Street. They were good guys, though, and raised $480,000 for us from twenty-four people they knew, such as doctors and dentists. Some were big-time investors, such as Joe McNay at Endowment Management & Research and Michael Winton at The Winton Family Foundation. Joe would join the Board and become a significant contributor. For one thing, he asked, "Where's the recurring revenue?" There was not any. That's when I created the Mandatory Annual Support Fee, the first in the industry and a very important source of revenue. However, at the last minute, the deal could not close because one investor dropped out. Sol came up with the necessary money, and he said it would turn out to be the best investment that he had ever made in his life. Sol was a very nice and generous guy in lots of ways.

However, eventually, my company would need more money, and we went to see Ted Rosen, who kept moving on to new investment banking companies. We sat in his office and listened while he turned down someone on the phone who had a company that had been profitable for a hundred years. It was clear that there would not be any more money for us. We would have to go home and figure out how to survive. Things were very tough on Wall Street at the time.

Cullinane Board members, management, and spouses on the floor of the NYSE watch first trade of company stock on ticker.

"For the first time, we demonstrated that a lot of money could be made with software."

Actual Ticker Tape

NEW YORK STOCK EXCHANGE

My company would get to a point where it had only $500 in the bank left and payroll due that day of $8,500 when a check for, literally, $8,500 came in that morning. We were going out of business. However, with some very imaginative marketing, we survived and then prospered. For example, we had only one product, a report generator called Culprit. It was not selling very well to IT departments. However, I noted that some auditors were using it, so I got a brochure from Arthur Anderson about audit software. Our Culprit report generator matched the requirements of an audit software system very well. So, I came up with a special version for auditors and gave it a different name called EDP Auditor. My technical staff said, "You cannot do that. It is the same system." I said, "We'll see." The first customer to buy EDP Auditor was a bank that had already bought Culprit, the First National Bank of Chicago. They did because we provided many special support services for auditors that were very important to them, such as independence of the audit, EDP Auditors User Group, a library of audit routines, etc. In fact, the auditors, who were non-programmers, would produce reports so fast that they would embarrass their IT departments into buying the Culprit version. It was key to our turning the corner.

Then we got into database software, and things took off. This led us to become the first financially successful software products company in the computer industry. We would be the first to go public, be listed on the New York Stock Exchange, and reach a $1 billion valuation. Everyone in my company had stock options, which were unique for the time, and did very well. For example, our stock came out at $20 and reached $800 per share. It was the most successful stock of any high-tech company from 1978 to 1985.

The day the company was to be listed on the NYSE, we chartered an Amtrak Club Car to pick us up at the Route 128 railroad station and take us to New York City. This included the Board of Directors and their spouses and senior management. They all watched the ticker tape above the trading floor of the NYSE, knowing that this trade was originating in London and was going around the world at the same moment. It would be the first trade of the day. It was all quite impressive. Also, everyone in the industry was watching us. For the first time, we demonstrated that a lot of money could be made with software.

A Board meeting of Cullinane Corporation (Cullinet Software, Inc.) Seated left to right are company executives Frank Chisholm, Bob Goldman, Phyllis Swersky, Board members George White and Pat Grant. Standing left to right are Board members David Rubin, Bobby Orr, Dick Bloch, John Cullinane, Joe McNay, Sol Manber, and Bill Eidson.

IT ALMOST DIDN'T HAPPEN

It all sounds great, but it came very close to not happening. IBM introduced a new computer six months after we went public and told every mutual customer and prospect that our database management system did not run on its new computer and that they would be out of the mainstream of all IBM database applications in the future. Every customer went into a panic, and every prospect went on hold. We were in big, big trouble. You never want to have a public offering and have a down quarter two quarters later. Many investors will be very unhappy, and worse, you will be on the receiving end of class action lawsuits, not a happy experience. In trying to calm our customer and prospect base, I visited a number of them in New Jersey one day with Bob Goldman, our VP of Technical Development. However, the weather was so bad that our plane home was delayed at Newark, so I decided to rent a car and drive home. It was pouring rain, but I do not remember anything about the drive from Newark to New Haven. Not a thing. Then it hit me. The light went on.

"I learned that it is much harder to sell the sales force than the customers and prospects."

The solution was our new Integrated Dictionary. We would move the sales focus off the database management system to the Integrated Data Dictionary and put IBM on the defensive. IBM had a dictionary but not an integrated one. This was key. However, we had to get the new sales message out very fast to customers and prospects, including that our database management system did indeed run-on IBM's new computer. Bob just had to change one instruction. So, Bob and I went on the road to present this at seminars to customers and prospects, and it worked. Our sales force took note of this. Incidentally, I learned that it is much harder to sell the sales force than the customers and prospects.

On the way home from one trip, we put it together in a sales format using my sales template and distributed slide presentations to all our salespeople, and insisted they use it "as is." The result was that we made our numbers for the fourth quarter, an incredible accomplishment. If we had not done this, no one would have ever been on the floor of the New York Stock Exchange watching the first trade of the day in Cullinane Corporation stock on the ticker tape.

This B-52 bomber was in a database maintained by my company's software.

THE STRATEGIC AIR COMMAND (SAC)

When major clients were considering buying my company's database software, they would often ask me to meet with the top information technology person in their company before they made their final decision. This was the case with the Strategic Air Command (SAC). I was asked to come to its headquarters in Omaha, Nebraska, to meet with General Evans, head of all information technology for SAC.

I was met at the gate by one of General Evans' aides. He said, "Before you give your presentation, I have a slide presentation about what we plan to use your software for." To my utter amazement, it was to control all SR-71 and U2 spy flights worldwide. All the sorties of B-52s carry nuclear bombs and everything else the Air Force had to fire at an enemy. This would be in one database. The second database contained everything an enemy might have that the Air Force would want to keep track of if it had to destroy them, such as submarines. By the time he was finished with his presentation, I had thought, this is the first line of defense of the United States! I had not bargained on this!

"Look, if your software doesn't work, now is the time to admit it and get the hell out of here!"

As I walked to the conference room to meet General Evans, I could hear *The Star-Spangled Banner* playing in my head. In the conference room with General Evans were thirteen Colonels with lots of ribbons on their chests. Before I could sit down, General Evans greeted me with, "Look, if your software doesn't work, now is the time to admit it and get the hell out of here!" I would have if it were the case. I then held up the slide carousel full of forty slides, which they eyed warily. I said, "I will only use five of them." They broke out into applause. The deal was done, and I had not even made the presentation yet.

This was about the size of the Halon demo canister.

THE WORST DEMONSTRATION

The computer industry has a well-earned reputation for disastrous demonstrations. One I witnessed took place at a conference on EDP Auditing in Atlanta, Georgia.

A sales type, a good ole boy from Georgia, began selling us the wonders of Halon systems after an unusual talk from our luncheon speaker, a bad omen. Halon is a gas that can put out a fire in a computer room without asphyxiating the people in the room. After an extremely long introduction to the magic of Halon, he was set to demonstrate it. He had placed a glassed-in telephone booth with lighted candles inside of it in the middle of this elegant ballroom. He then invited the conference organizer to stand in the telephone booth to demonstrate the effectiveness of the Halon system. It would put out the candles but not hurt him in any way. As the Halon system came on, it produced a fog, and the man disappeared. Then, there was a huge bang or explosion. Nobody knew what it was, but as the fog dissipated

"As the Halon system came on, it produced a fog, and the man disappeared. Then, there was a huge bang or explosion."

in the booth, the man's face reappeared, and he looked terrified. Then, we all seemed to look up at the ceiling of the ballroom at the same time to see that there was a big hole in the ceiling. One could even see bent girders that held up the roof. What had happened was that the canister of Halon that had been bolted into the side of the booth had become, literally, a missile. Fortunately, it went straight up and not sideways because if it did, it could have killed or injured many people in the room.

The salesman tried to explain this unfortunate demonstration with a lot of double talk. Nothing he could say could change the fact that, in my experience, this was the worst demonstration I had ever seen in the computer industry or would ever see.

However, our day was not over. We were at the conference in the first place to conduct a sales seminar for prospects, only no prospects showed up, not one. We had to pack up all the brochures, etc., and head back to Boston, a bad day on the road. When I got back home, I would sometimes visit our big computer center and take note of the huge canisters of Halon concealed behind the walls. There must have been enough Halon in them to send us to the moon.

These are the four Americans who got to The Royal and Ancient Golf Club of St. Andrews in the Bentley - Peter Lacaillade, Paul Birmingham, John Cullinane and Carlyle Baker

Bentley Town Car

Rolls Royce Cullinan Arctic SUV

THE BENTLEY

Rolls Royce Motor Car Company installed my company's manufacturing system. It was hugely successful. Every Rolls Royce and Bentley would now be made with my company's software and probably still is.

The Rolls Royce IT Director and the top person responsible for the project asked to meet with me at a company User Group meeting held in Switzerland. It was a very emotional meeting as he and his top aide thanked me profusely for the success of the project and the incredibly positive impact it had on their careers. With much emotion, he said if there was anything he could do for me, he would be more than happy to do so.

A few months later, I was invited to go on a golf trip beginning at Royal Dornoch Golf Club in Northern Scotland. I remembered his offer and thought, why not ask for a Rolls Royce loaner? He said, no problem. A couple of days before we left for Scotland, he called to say a Rolls Royce was not available, but would a Bentley Town Car do? Of course, it would.

"Every Rolls Royce and Bentley would now be made with my company's software."

When we landed at Inverness, a very small airport in Northern Scotland, I was greeted by a chauffeur who handed me the keys to the Bentley plus an official tie. He said the car was outside in the parking lot. I asked him where he was going. He said he was getting on the plane and flying back to London, about 600 miles away. I was astounded. I thought there would be some Bentley agency nearby. I would never have asked for a loaner under such circumstances.

My lasting impression is of these four Americans riding in this big Bentley trailed by this little taxi carrying our golf clubs as we headed to our hotel on a narrow road in the Scottish Highlands. It was like we were Rajs in India. Then, on to the R&A, courtesy of a member friend.

Rolls Royce came out with a new car a couple of years ago. It's their first SUV, and it is named Cullinan. Too bad they did not have it when we were going to Scotland. A Cullinane driving a Cullinan. That would have made for some interesting possibilities, such as a doorman saying, "Mr. Cullinane, your Cullinan is here."

This is a LISA with a mouse that was in my office linked to a Palo Alto data center with Steve Jobs there.

STEVE JOBS

To much acclaim, Apple Computer and Microsoft burst on the scene in the early eighties. This was when most people in the media believed that the computer and related software industry began. There had been very little coverage of main-frame software companies such as mine even though we were very famous in the industry. Once I dropped into a PC show featuring many new companies promoting related products and services. No one in a booth there knew who I was or recognized my company's name. Change was in the air.

Dan Bricklin, very famous in his own right for creating the first spreadsheet system, wanted to introduce me to Bill Gates at a Massachusetts Software Council meeting. Dan was surprised when Bill did not know who I was. However, the PC world was like another world. They were going to do away with all those main frame computers and give everyone their own computer. Only it was not going to happen that way. For example, my company developed breakthrough communications technology, allowing the linkage of personal computers to IBM mainframe computer databases

"Steve was going to save Apple with the LISA, which was designed for corporate America. We had the corporate customer base that Apple was after, so it was a perfect fit."

for the first time. It was the earliest Cloud technology. As a result, we agreed with Apple Computer to link our database software residing on an IBM computer to Steve Jobs' new LISA computer. Steve was going to save Apple with the LISA, which was designed for corporate America. We had the corporate customer base that Apple was after, so it was a perfect fit.

To introduce this great new technology, we created a video of me using a mouse with a LISA computer in my office in Westwood, Massachusetts, just like Steve Jobs is using in the picture. I would download information from our database system running on an IBM mainframe computer in a Palo Alto, California, data center to the LISA. Steve Jobs and the Chairman of the Board of Apple were videoed in the IBM center, the first time Steve Jobs was ever in such a center. It was also the first time I had ever used a mouse. Unfortunately, very few corporations, or anyone for that matter, wanted to buy the very expensive LISA. Even Steve Jobs cannot be right all the time.

Bobby Orr at Northeastern Honorary Degree ceremony and giving commencement speech at right.

BOBBY ORR

I first met Bobby Orr when I was hitting a golf shot at the 17th hole at Weston Country Club in a charity golf tournament. I was shocked to look up and see that Bobby was watching me do something. After I mishit the shot, I asked him why he was following our group. He said one of the members was a good friend of his who had just lost his wife, and he was along to cheer him up.

At the time, I was thinking about adding some new members to my Board versus the same old bankers or lawyers. I thought, why not Bobby Orr? He checked out well, so I put him and another unusual choice, Gerard Doherty, on the Board at the same time. Bobby once said to a writer that the most nervous he ever was in his life was when he went to the first Board meeting at Cullinet.

"As one astute observer said, if you put five Bobby Orr's on the ice with five Wayne Gretzky's, the Bobby Orr's would win 10-0. I think he is right."

I was once on a flight with him to a User Group meeting in Las Vegas and, ironically, they were showing "The Natural." I was watching for a while and thought no one is that good. Then I thought, I am sitting next to The Natural! Bobby was watching it intently. I wondered what he was thinking.

Bobby once gave one of his Bruins jerseys to a Boston radio station to auction off for charity. Some of my employees bought it and gave it to me as a gift. It sat in a drawer for many years in a plastic wrap. It was not doing anyone any good, so I put it up for auction. It turned out to be the real deal. I used the proceeds to do some good, but in Bobby's name. After all, he's the one who made it so valuable with his blood, sweat, and ability.

In the opinion of his peers, Bobby Orr was the greatest player ever to play the game. Others would say, what about Wayne Gretzky? As one astute observer said, if you put five Bobby Orr's on the ice with five Wayne Gretzky's, the Bobby Orr's would win 10-0. I think he is right.

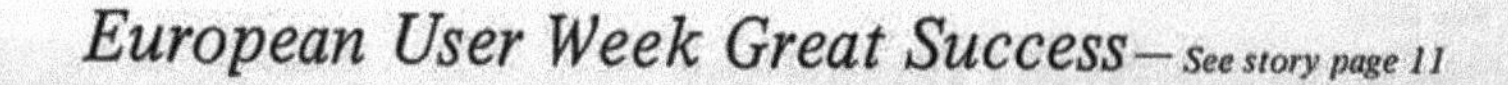

European User Week Great Success — *See story page 11*

CULLINANE REPORT

Cullinane Database Systems, Inc., 400 Blue Hill Drive, Westwood, Mass. 02090

Nearly 1000 attend in Las Vegas, Rome

User Week '80 biggest and best yet

Las Vegas, Nevada — Computer software users from all over North America, Europe and Scandinavia gathered in Las Vegas, Nevada and Rome, Italy for Cullinane's recent "User Week '80" conference.

Held at the Las Vegas Hilton, Domestic User Week attracted more than 600 Cullinane software clients, representing some 300 American and Canadian firms. The participants, accompanied by more than 200 guests, attended a week of workshops, technical sessions, demonstrations, user group meetings and product overviews.

Especially well-received were the case histories presented by users themselves, which dealt with topics ranging from software performance analyses and control guidelines to applications for manufacturing, education and finance.

New name, location, services

Founder and President John J. Cullinane opened the company's fourth domestic User Week with an outstanding corporate forecast, a discussion of Cullinane's new services and product line and a brief history of the company's impressive growth.

"We're building new headquarters and getting a new name," he said, referring to the company's new corporate headquarters in Westwood, Massachusetts and its new name, Cullinane Database Systems, Inc. "We're developing an extensive new line of products and services for our clients and we've just completed a $15 million stock offering to finance it all.

"We're strongly positioned for the future—and with our exceptional cash position and no debt, we'll continue our 13-year record of success."

Proceeds from the stock offering will be used to acquire, develop and market application software packages, Mr. Cullinane said. Application software is more "task-oriented" than conventional packaged software, helping users address specific tasks such as inventory control, general ledger, accounts payable and receivable and numerous operations in banking, manufacturing and finance.

Mr. Cullinane discussed another new

(Continued on page 2)

Cullinane User Week in Las Vegas

Cullinet User Week in Boston

USER WEEKS

Cullinane Corporation User Weeks would become the event of the year. It was something that I controlled and changed each year as appropriate. Everything would point to it, such as new software products and/or releases. It started small in Boston and just grew to thousands of attendees. Ours was different from all other software companies in that we charged a good deal of money but provided a lot in return, including free education classes for each attendee. This is how customers could justify coming. From our perspective, they went home more knowledgeable about the use of our products. Also, our salespeople would bring their best prospects, and they would always go home sold. We were not afraid to mix prospects with actual users. They were our best salespeople.

"Our salespeople would bring their best prospects, and they would always go home sold. We were not afraid to mix prospects with actual users. They were our best salespeople."

On Wednesday evening, we would have a big gala featuring groups like "The Temptations." Many other software companies would copy us. User Weeks would always be at the best hotel we could find that could accommodate our requirements. When you bring thousands of customers to a city as we did, they will do anything. This included putting your name up on billboards on the way in from the airports or even on the Great White Way in Las Vegas. For example, once when my taxi pulled up to the Hilton, I saw my name up in lights with the stars of the day. I was shocked but impressed I might add. Then, the taciturn cabbie asked, "Who is this Cullinane, anyway?" I paused for a moment, wondering what to say. Then I said, "It's me." He turned and stared at me to see if I was putting him on. What's ironic is that after a few days, the signs start coming down, and nobody knows who you are by Thursday. Martha Burnham, my assistant, confirmed this. When the User Week she ran was over, she, the most important woman of the week, had to wait an hour for her car while sitting on the curb.

The plane leaving Bremen was surrounded by military with machine guns as we waited to take off. A shipment of gold for London was being loaded on the plane, but it was still unsettling. It reminded me of the movie *Casablanca*.

SELLING IN GERMANY

Jürgen Schoon showed up at my office one day when my company was very small. He wanted to represent us in Germany and sell our Culprit report generator package. He certainly would be an impressive-looking representative. Also, he would become very successful at it.

Our first sales meeting in Germany was with the IT Director of an aircraft manufacturer in Bremen. I thought of all the German I knew, which was limited to John Kennedy's speech in Berlin and WWII movies. So, I started the meeting with, "Ich bin ein Amerikaner, nein sprechen sie Deutsch." The IT Director's response was, "Ah, you speak German! So many Americans come here, and they cannot speak German. How do they expect to do business with us?" I wonder what I said wrong, but we got the business.

Jürgen Schoon

Betty Grant, a former company sales executive, Joan & Jon Nackerud

Jim Baker

THE SMARTEST PEOPLE

I once introduced Neil Rudenstine, President of Harvard, at an event, saying that I had thought about applying for the Presidency of Harvard. The first reason was that I had a wife who was very good at fundraising and, second, I was used to running a company where everyone who worked there thought that they were smarter than I was.

It was true. Just about everyone in my company was smarter than I was. For example, Jim Baker, a key VP, was a member of the Honor Society at MIT in Electrical Engineering and a Ph.D. candidate at Harvard in Philosophy. They do not get much smarter than this. I once asked him what sort of a mind he thought he had. He said a B+. I asked him who he thought was an A. He said, John Von Neumann, the great mathematician. Bill Linn, our regional VP in Atlanta, had a Ph.D. in Computer Science. Nobody was smarter or harder working than our Polish American VPs from Chicago, Flip Filipowski and Ray Nawara. Jon Nackerud was another example. Everyone was smart.

I met Jon Nackerud at Transamerica in San Francisco when I gave a sales presentation on our Culprit product. It was a very technical group, and I did not know the answers to any of their very technical questions, but Jon amazingly knew them all. Jon's boss even shouted at him to let me answer the questions. However, I was very appreciative that he bailed me out.

Eventually, Jon would join the company and become responsible for the West Coast as a Vice President. He invited me to come to the first meeting he set up with a large group of prospects and customers. In introducing me, he said that when they formed the company, they named it Cullinane Corporation. Then they went looking for someone named Cullinane to run it, and I was the first one they found. I laughed at the audacity, but that was Jon. It would not be the last time he would be irreverent but, always, in a very humorous way.

Thus, I was surrounded by these brilliant technicians, and I was a non-technician. I know some wondered what I did. I would say the company brought the best out of them and allowed them to prosper. As a result, the company was extraordinarily good at sales and technology, which was rare for a technology company, and we were well managed. That's why we succeeded so well.

Diddy and I at Longwood's 100th Anniversary

THE US PRO TENNIS CHAMPIONSHIP

Each year the US Pro Tennis Championship would be held at Longwood Cricket Club in Chestnut Hill, Massachusetts. It's a small but very pleasant and historic club with great focus on grass courts. All the world's great tennis players would show up. It was a very collegial affair, with the pros mingling with the members on the porch, etc. Arthur Ashe might be showering in the next stall, or Jimmy Connors might be hitting balls on the next court. My son, John, Jr., was a ball boy for a Björn Borg match and emulated his high lobs the next day. The championship was played on clay; it was its ultimate undoing.

One year there was a rain delay, and they were looking for someone to sponsor the necessary added day of the tournament on Monday night on PBS. Since I was planning on a public offering down the road, I thought this might not be a bad thing to sponsor. A lot of people in the financial world play tennis and would wonder what Cullinane Corporation was. I negotiated a deal under the stands on a rainy Friday night to sponsor the tournament. I would get a shared sponsorship on Sunday night

"I negotiated a deal under the stands on a rainy Friday night to sponsor the tournament. I would get a shared sponsorship on Sunday night with three other companies."

with three other companies. However, I would get sole sponsorship on Monday night, all for $25,000. It seemed like a good deal to me. Bud Collins, the great Boston Globe columnist and tennis expert, was the announcer. It was funny to listen to him because he quickly read off the three names of the other sponsors on Sunday night, which were all big-name corporations such as American Airlines. Then, when he came to Cullinane Corporation, I sensed what he was thinking, "Cullinane Corporation? What is that? Where did that come from? Nobody told me how to pronounce it." Then, there was a long pause, and he guessed it. He came close. In time, there would be no US Pro Tennis Championship anymore. None of the players wanted to play on clay with the US Open coming up in New York on a hard surface the next week.

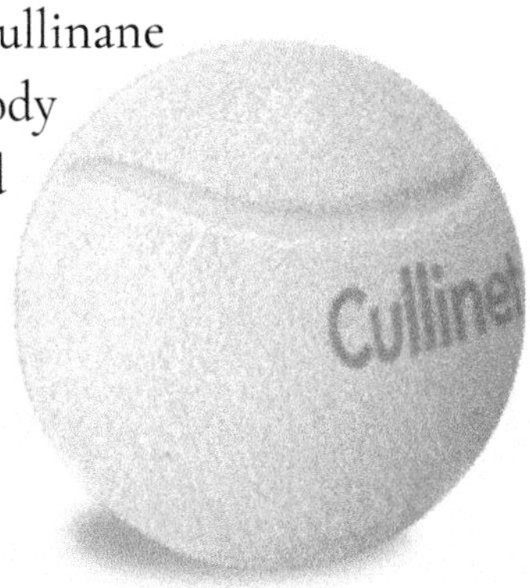

Cullinane Management Committee (l-r): Robert Goldman, President and Chairman of the Committee; Phyllis Swersky, Treasurer; Dr. William Linn, Sr. Vice President; and Frank Chisholm, Sr. Vice President..

THE PRESENTATION

Thanks to Henry McCance, Greylock Management invested in Cullinane Corporation. They bought my stock as a late-stage investor about a year before we went public. Later I was asked to make a presentation to Greylock's management team headed by Dan Gregory, Sr., and major Greylock investors such as Tom Watson, Jr., of IBM fame. This was a first for me, and it was a big deal to be invited.

I was driving up Rte. 128 on the way to the meeting, I looked out the rear-view mirror, and there was paper billowing behind me. What was that? It was my presentation. I had left the manilla folder on top of the car. Now, what was I going to do? When I told Dan why I had no presentation, he just laughed and told me that he was tired of listening to these formal presentations, anyhow. He told me to tell them what was going on, and I did, and it worked fine.

However, it was not quite like Frank Chisholm's presentations. Frank was our VP of Sales. I had managed to get us the opportunity to present our database management product, IDMS, to McGraw Hill's IT department, which was heavily biased in favor of IBM's IMS product. This was just before McGraw Hill would make its final decision. A few days earlier, Bob Goldman, VP of Technical Development, and I had gone to Detroit to make a sales presentation that worked. On the way back on the plane, we created a sales presentation based on it using my sales messaging template. On Thursday, I gave it to our media person, Logan Smith, and he had the slides ready on Monday. Thus, I was able to take the carousel of slides to New Jersey the next day for Frank to use. We met just as the meeting was about to start, so he had no time to prepare. He never even saw the slides. I smiled as he took a little extra time with each slide as he studied it. No one in the room would notice this, but I did because I knew he was seeing the slide for the first time. However, he presented each one perfectly, and we won the contract, the largest in the company's history up until that time. To me, it has always been the greatest presentation I have ever seen.

Ironically, we took these things for granted. That is just the way we did things, and I still marvel at our people's ability to do things on the fly. For example, Jim Baker would ask me one minute before he was to make a presentation at a User Week, "What do you want me to say?" Then he would do a beautiful job.

Golfing with Arnold Palmer (The King)

CHAPTER 4 | GOLFING

ARNOLD PALMER

Golfing with Arnold Palmer, courtesy of Win Hindle of DEC, was very daunting. When teeing off, thousands of people were staring back at you. This is quite an experience for any amateur. You know that there is the distinct possibility you could hit one of the people watching. President Ford, unfortunately, did it on a number of occasions while playing with Bob Hope.

We were playing at Nashawtuc Country Club in Concord, Massachusetts, an ideal course for Arnold at the time. Arnold teed off from the back tees, and we, amateurs, teed off from the front tees, and the distance between the two was about fifty yards. Arnold, unlike some professionals, is very pleasant to play with and very solicitous of the amateurs he is playing with. He made everyone feel relaxed. In my case, I hit an excellent drive off the tee, which was followed by a very good three wood. Arnie was very complimentary of it. It was followed by a perfectly hit pitching wedge with a large crowd around me that, unfortunately, landed just short of the green and plugged into the wet grass. However, Arnie told me I had a free lift. Ironically, all I had left on this Par 5 hole was a very short little pitch to the pin, maybe 10-15 feet. I missed it. I mean, I completely missed the ball! I wondered if anybody noticed or just thought it was a practice swing, but I truly missed it. How could I have done that with Arnie watching?

When I brought up flying, Arnold was much more interested in talking about flying his jet than golf. He loved to fly. He did tell a harrowing story about flying his Canadair jet from Hawaii to San Francisco. This distance was its outer range if given favorable tailwind conditions. He had favorable conditions when he took off, but the wind shifted to the nose of the plane just after passing the point of no return. This made for a couple of very dicey hours while they wondered if they were going to have to ditch off the California coast or not. They did make it to Carmel on fumes, he said. Unfortunately, however, our time together would be over, as thunderstorms would shut down the tournament, and Arnie was gone.

John, Diddy, President Clinton, Sandrine and John Jr.

Mikhail Baryshnikov was a pretty good golfer, too.

PRESIDENT BILL CLINTON

I was attending a meeting with Bill and Hillary Clinton at White Oaks Plantation on St. Mary's River, which separates Florida from Georgia. At the meeting, a young man asked if I would like to play golf with the President. If so, his instructions were to meet the President at the Pro Shop. The plantation had a private nine-hole golf course, golf pros, and all the equipment you needed, free.

In the small room off the pro shop waiting for President Clinton was another golfer, Mikhail Baryshnikov. He ran a ballet studio at the plantation. He was very friendly and personable. In conversation, I happened to bring up Jimmy Cagney, whom he knew, and his dancing style in the movie "Yankee Doodle Dandy." Mikhail then burst into a spontaneous imitation of Jimmy doing his dance in the movie to an audience of one. It was incredible to watch him perform. He was also an avid golfer.

"Mikhail then burst into a spontaneous imitation of Jimmy (Cagney) doing his dance in the movie to an audience of one. It was incredible to watch him perform. He was also a good golfer."

Playing golf with Bill Clinton was a "happening." First, there were eight people in our group, the only group on the course. Some golfers were new to the game and very tense. He would give each player advice after every missed shot. It took about 45 minutes to play the first hole, but I did not care. Incidentally, he hits the ball a long way, if somewhat errantly sometimes. I smiled after he once hit his drive into a pond. He noticed it, and I could tell he was annoyed with me. I explained that I was not smiling because of the errant shot he hit but because it was so evident that he got so much enjoyment out of the game. I could understand why big-name pros such as Greg Norman liked to play golf with him.

Bill Russell receiving the Presidential Medal of Freedom.

BILL RUSSELL

Bill's lawyer, now Ambassador Barry White, asked me to play golf with Bill. He was looking for some advice on what he might do in the future to generate revenue, etc. First, we played golf. I found that Bill had a great sense of humor and is very competitive, like all great athletes.

On the 12th hole at The Country Club in Brookline, a very short par three, I hit what looked like a perfect shot. It was high in the air, landed on the green, and ended up about six feet from the hole. However, I knew that I had hit a real clunker that just looked good, but who in this group would know? Then, I heard from the back of me, "Nice miss." Russell knew! On the 18th, I sank a very long putt to tie the match as his partner. He was so enthusiastic; you would think we had just won an NBA title together.

"Bill was a delightful person to play golf with, and I was honored to have had the opportunity to play with him. He played at a sixteen handicap, the same as Baryshnikov."

Not long afterward, I was at Senator Ted Kennedy's funeral service. There was a long wait for the service to begin, and I noticed that Bill was close by with his daughter. I introduced myself and said he might not remember me, but we had recently played golf at TCC. He said, "Of course, I remember you; you white guys don't all look alike to me." I must have had the right reaction because he burst into that booming, wild cackle of a laugh he has. You could hear it all over the church.

Bill was a delightful person to play golf with, and I was honored to have had the opportunity to play with him. He played at a sixteen handicap, the same as Baryshnikov.

(l-r) John Cullinane, Joe Tierney, good friend Charlie Fox and Mayor Menino (far right) playing at Diddy's Black & White on Green Golf Tournament.

MAYOR TOM MENINO

I first got to know Tom Menino as a member of the Park Street Forum, a think tank founded by Father Quinn. Father Quinn would cook breakfast for the members, and Tom Menino, a City Councilor, would bring the donuts. He rarely said anything, but Tom Menino was one of the most astute politicians I ever met, right up there with Bill Clinton. When Mayor Flynn was appointed Ambassador to Rome, Tom ran for Mayor and won. Many in the business community thought I was clairvoyant for supporting him, but by then I had been working on the Boston Public Library Foundation with him. It became clear to me that if Tom Menino ever got a chance to run for Mayor, he would win. He had friends everywhere and, most importantly, they could vote. Angela, his wife, was a big part of it as well. They worked as a team. He would become a very popular Mayor.

"Tom loved to play golf. He would always play in Diddy's Black & White on Green Golf Tournament at Franklin Park."

Tom loved to play golf. He would always play in Diddy's Black & White on Green Golf Tournament at Franklin Park. One day he invited me to play with him, former Boston Mayor Kevin White, and former Massachusetts State Treasurer Bob Crane at Franklin Park. Mayor White had advanced Alzheimer's at the time, and Bob had been very kind and solicitous to him for years. Mayor White was in very good health otherwise and could hit the ball and putt very well. Bob just had to tell him when and where to hit the ball and where to putt it, etc. I would hit the drives for the foursome in a scramble. I hit a good drive on the 16th hole, and the ball ended up about a pitching wedge from the hole. Mayor White hit his shot and, miraculously, it went into the hole with a big crowd around the green watching. They all cheered him as he approached the green. Ironically, the one thing that Mayor White could react to was being recognized. Thus, wherever Bob Crane was with Mayor White, he would always encourage anybody around to call him Mr. Mayor. With the shot, Mayor White created it for himself. It was a very memorable moment.

The 33rd
Ryder Cup
Matches
The Country Club
Brookline, Massachusetts

THE RYDER CUP CORPORATE HOSPITALITY

In 1999, The Ryder Cup was held at The Country Club in Brookline, Massachusetts. John Cornish, who Chaired the event, asked me to head up the Corporate Hospitality Committee, which I had done for the US Open in 1988. The Corporate Hospitality at the Open was extraordinarily successful, but The Ryder Cup would be ten times as successful. We raised more money from tents and tables than had ever been raised in a golf tournament, perhaps to this day. However, what was unique at the time was that The Country Club shared this largess with local communities. For example, the Club provided tickets to the City of Boston for Mayor Menino's Ryder Cup Week at Franklin Park. The Club helped sell these tickets and raise $1.5 million to fund future youth activities in the City. Many Boston CEOs who had played in Diddy's Black & White on Green Tournament helped because they learned that Franklin Park was a beautiful venue with a great golf course. Also, companies such as Coca-Cola that did not have exclusive agreements with PGA America could participate in The Ryder Cup.

Similarly, the Town of Brookline received an extra $500,000 for youth activities in addition to the $5 million it got for services. Also, the Club reached out to the minority business community to create opportunities for it. This was not easy because PGA America has contracts for everything with national vendors. Finally, there was not a single complaint from any corporate subscriber the whole week. They were all thrilled to be part of such a historic event and with such a remarkable finish regardless of where their tents or tables were located.

One of the reasons was that The 1999 Ryder Cup was, arguably, the greatest golf event in the history of America. The American team was way down after Saturday's matches, and the chances of winning did not look good. I was a Standard Bearer for the Woods/Coltart match and, by the time they played, you could sense when looking at the leader board that something remarkable was underway. Eventually, Justin Leonard would sink a difficult 40 ft. putt on the famed 17th hole to win it all. I do not think I had ever seen anyone make that putt before. The putt was moving so fast that it might have been off the green if it did not go in. The great golf announcer and player Johnny Miller said it was the greatest putt in Ryder Cup history. The golfing gods were with the Americans on that Sunday, big time.

Ed Forry, Joe Corcoran, Father McDonnell, Paul Donahue and Bob Quinn.

Peter Barber

ST. AUGUSTINE'S

I was hitting golf balls on the driving range at The Country Club in Brookline when Peter Barber, a fellow member, came over and asked if I would play in and support a golf tournament he was organizing to raise money for St. Augustine's. It would be played at Franklin Park in Dorchester. I said sure, but I was somewhat surprised because St. Augustine's was a very poor parish in South Boston run by a remarkable priest I knew very well, Father Thomas McDonnell. He would always do the convocation of any event that Diddy or I chaired, beginning with JFK Library Foundation dinners for foreign dignitaries such as the Prime Minister of Pakistan, Benazir Bhutto. He was outstanding in this role. PM Bhutto listened very closely to what he said and was very impressed with his view of the similarities between Christianity and Islam. However, I was puzzled that Peter would even know Father McDonnell and be supportive of St Augustine's Parish, but that was just a passing thought.

"This event isn't for St. Augustine's Catholic Church in South Boston; it's for St Augustine's Episcopal Monastery in Harvard Square!"

Regardless, I showed up on the appointed day at Franklin Park but did not see anyone I knew, including Father McDonnell. Eventually, I went over to Peter and asked him, "Where is Father McDonnell?" He said, "Who?" I said, "Father McDonnell from St. Augustine's Catholic Church in South Boston." Peter replied, "This event isn't for St. Augustine's Catholic Church in South Boston; it's for St Augustine's Episcopal Monastery in Harvard Square!"

Afterward, I apologized to Father McDonnell. I had given his money to the Episcopalians. Later you will see a picture of me playing golf with Peter Lynch and Tip O'Neill. I am wearing a very nice green Episcopalian shirt that would easily pass in South Boston that I got at this event.

THE BOSTON GLOBE • WEDNESDAY, SEPTEMBER 10, 1997

NAMES & FACES

BY SUSAN BICKELHAUPT AND MAUREEN DEZELL

HITTING THE LINKS - From left, John Cullinane, Barbara Paige, Fletcher "Flash" Wiley, and Mayor Tom Menino were among 160 corporate, academic, and political bigwigs who played golf in the fifth annual Black & White on Green tourney at Franklin Park yesterday. Other golfers included the Rev. J. Donald Monan of Boston College, former Gov. Mike Dukakis, businessman Ron Homer, Eric Turner of State Street Bank, Paul Foster of Reebok, and entrepreneur Earl Tate. They raised $60,000 for Black & White's caddie scholarship fund. Golfers and nonplaying pols Ralph Martin, Dianne Wilkerson, and Peggy Davis-Mullen gathered for a barbecue beneath a tent after the tournament, where jokes and jabs were the order of the afternoon. Bob Mahoney, president of Citizens Bank, said of his game with Wiley and Monan, "Flash couldn't use half his vocabulary because Father Monan was there." Wiley, for his part, said he was keeping quiet to allow "Father Moran to pray over my golf game."

BLACK & WHITE ON GREEN

My team won Diddy's Black & White on Green Golf Tournament one year. As soon as my name was announced as one of the team members, some in the audience started to boo. This was because I was the husband of the event organizer. The booing seemed unfair since we had won the tournament fair and square. The booing continued as this picture was taken when we received our trophy from Gale Sayers, Chairman of the Tournament that year and football Hall of Famer. On my team were two of Cullinane Corporation's earliest and key Vice Presidents, Tom Meurer and Bill Casey, along with Ed Owens. That is why everyone is smiling so much, even Gale Sayers, although Tom, I think, is looking at the crowd a little warily. You could not pose it. It did not bother us, though, as you can tell. Booing was just another form of appreciation.

Another time I was playing in the tournament on a foggy day in a threesome when a man appeared out of the deep mist carrying a golf bag. He asked if he could join us. We said sure and asked his name. He said, "Bobby Jones." Only, he was a Black Bobby Jones. Then, he proceeded to play like the White Bobby Jones. It was like we were in some Hollywood golf movie such as "Bagger Vance" without realizing it. Who was he? Actually, he was the Franklin Park Club Champion and had been sent out to join us, and he really could play.

Ed Owens, John Cullinane, Gale Sayers, Tom Meurer, and Bill Casey.

Peter Lacaillade's gift trophy

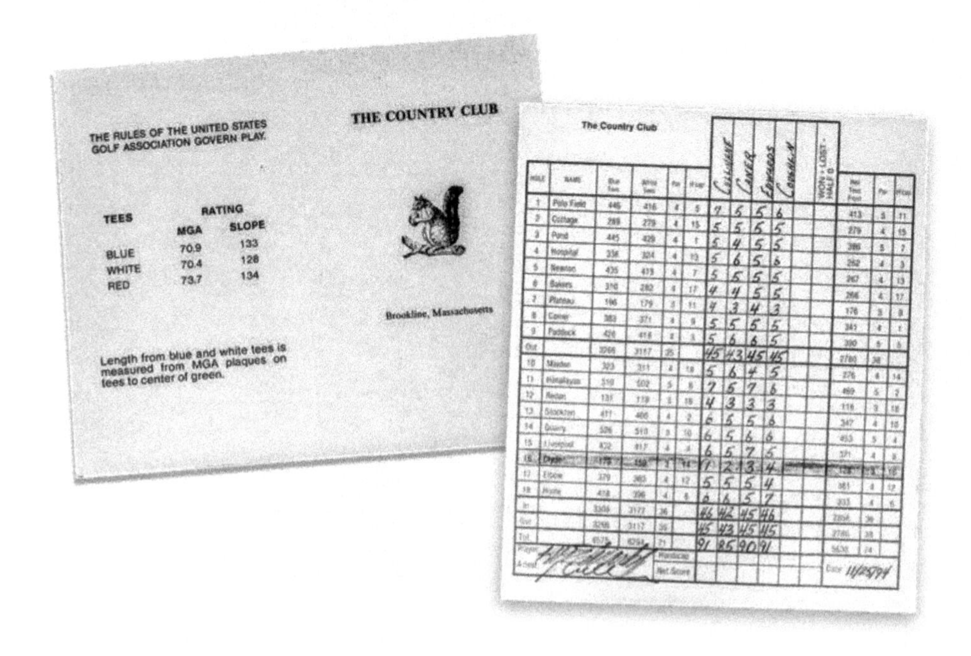

A HOLE IN ONE

You have to be very lucky to get a hole in one. However, in my case, I was unusually lucky. On a Wednesday, Peter Lacaillade, a good friend, bought a hole in one trophy for a surprise birthday party Diddy was having for me on a Saturday night in Chatham. He even had it engraved, which was a nice touch, but without a date. Thursday was Thanksgiving Day, which was my original birthday date. On Friday, I got the hole in one on the 16th at The Country Club in Brookline just in time for the party.

The second unusual thing was that it was a 1234 foursome. In other words, I got a 1; an opponent got a 2, my partner got a 3, and our other opponent got a 4. According to a good friend and golf expert, Charlie Fox, this was very rare. In fact, a group did it at Brae Burn Country Club, and they were known as the 1234 Foursome for the rest of their lives. We received no recognition whatsoever. However, I wish the

"This is late November. So, the ball in the trophy is not the real ball I used. I could not put such an awful looking ball in a trophy. It would be bad for my image."

member that got the 2 was still alive so that I could remind him of it. He was very competitive, and it was probably the first time in his life that he ever lost a par 3 hole with a 2. Another postscript is I had just found the ball I used to get the hole in one. It was a cheap ball and pretty scuffed, but with a club logo. Remember, this is late November. So, the ball in the trophy is not the real ball I used. I could not put such an awful looking ball in a trophy. It would be bad for my image.

Years later, I would send this story to Dr. Eric O'Brien, a renowned Irish golfer and good friend who was recovering from an operation. He thought the 1234 part was "incredible." Diddy believes the timing of getting the hole in one is what is incredible, but she is not a golfer. Either way, it was incredible.

This story appeared in the summer edition of the UK's *Golf Quarterly* known as the home of elegant, witty writing on golf for amateurs.

John Cullinane, good friend Bill Deery, Will McDonough, and fourth golfer.

RFK MEMORIAL GOLF TOURNAMENT

Every year Ethel Kennedy would host the Robert F. Kennedy Memorial Golf Tournament at the Hyannisport Golf Club. It had everything—loads of big-name celebrities, terrific prizes like Boston Whalers on every hole and a great course. In fact, I won a very fancy and expensive exercise chair (that even vibrated) by being closest to the hole despite my putt being 30 ft away.

"It had everything—loads of big-name celebrities, terrific prizes like Boston Whalers on every hole and a great course."

That was the year we thought our team won the golf tournament. It included Will McDonough, a famous *Boston Globe* sports columnist, my very good friend, Bill Deery, and one other. However, after a very long deliberation, it was determined that we didn't win it. Instead, we tied with Bill Van Faasen's team that included Michael Kennedy, and there would have to be a playoff. We had no chance because Bill Van Faasen was a great golfer. However, on the 18th hole, Michael Kennedy, who was not a golfer, sank an incredible 40 ft downhill putt to win. This took place in front of a vast and cheering crowd on the porch and around the green. It seemed like a fitting end, all things considered.

Dr. Richard Scott

NINE HOLES & WINTER GOLF

I decided to play only nine holes, which only takes an hour and a half. This leaves lots of time for other activities. Others like it, too. As a result, I have nine-hole matches that have been going on for years with the same players, such as Peter Lacaillade and John Hamill in Chatham. The matches almost always go down to the last putt because Peter and John are very competitive. In Boston, I have been playing equally competitive nine-hole matches for years with Dr. Richard Scott, a world-renowned knee surgeon. We continue to play in the winter because we belong to a course with nine holes that stays open. Global warming makes it possible to play many days during the winter months. I wonder why so many courses close down for the winter when they are perfectly playable. We have been joined by others for some very competitive matches. If the temperature is around 40 degrees, and there is no wind and some sun, it is OK to play golf. Properly bundled, it is pretty warm, and sometimes a ball destined for a pond in the summertime bounces off the ice and onto a green.

Recently, I was put to the test regarding winter golf. Sir Martin Smith, a hardy Brit, was eager to play Eastward Ho! in Chatham after a two-year absence caused by Covid restrictions. Eastward Ho! stays open all year and is perfectly maintained. The forecast was for a frigid and windy day, a fatal combination, but I thought I would at least give it a try. As we walked to a tee, a woman in a car stopped, rolled down her window, and asked, "Do you realize it's 29 degrees out?" However, the winds died, and the sun was bright and quite warm in the valleys. The views were spectacular, too. We could see blue skies, blue ocean, sandy beaches with people walking on them, green pine trees, and greenish grass. I could not help but think that this is exactly how it looks in the summertime, and we were the only ones on this beautiful course.

However, this was child's play compared to playing Royal Dublin Golf Club with then Executive Dean of the Kennedy School, Richard Cavanagh, and Kurt Campbell, a faculty member. They were determined to play regardless of the weather. We teed off when it was snowing and a twenty-mile-per-hour wind in our faces. We turned the corner and played the last nine holes coming in with the wind and the sleet at our backs. This was a significant improvement over going out, as bad as it sounds. The Irish know what they are talking about when they say, "May the wind be always at your back."

The Holy Grail of Golf

THE HOLY GRAIL

I have greatly admired and even envied golfers who could hit the ball well and consistently. How did they do it? Were they born with this gift or not? So, I looked for the Holy Grail of Golf for fifty years. I was about to give up out of frustration when I decided to try and simplify the swing by just taking it straight back and finishing high, with no body turn. It seemed to work very well. A few months later, while watching the Golf Channel and Moe Norman, I realized that I had stumbled onto his swing as the most accurate hitter of the golf ball ever. However, I still had not found the Holy Grail of Golf. Tom Meurer, an old friend, gave me a driver he had in his garage, and it helped. However, I noticed that if I kept my eye on the ball, it did wonders. I even put the ball on the tee so I could focus on the logo to help and then took a couple of deep breaths to relax. This, I found, was key. It allowed me to watch the club hit the ball or be very close to it. It is that

"The Holy Grail of Golf is simply watching the ball while hitting it. Plus a full backswing."

simple, in my opinion. For example, I once hit 41 straight fairways with the driver. Golfers would say that this is impossible, but I did it, and 50% of the drives were at Eastward Ho!. It is a very hilly course with sloped fairways where balls hit down the middle of the fairway can run into the rough. However, the problem was that I could not do it with the other clubs. Imagine hitting fourteen drives in the fairway but no second shots; very frustrating. So, for years I looked for the Holy Grail with the other clubs. I tried all kinds of different swings on the practice range, and they all worked great but never on the course. Then, recently, I tried taking the club back more on the course and I was startled with the results. I think I have found The Holy Grail of Golf. Taking the club farther back eliminated "short arming" the swing. It also allowed me to concentrate on looking at the ball just as I did with the driver. It works great as long as I watch the ball when I hit it. I am now convinced that The Holy Grail of Golf is simply watching the ball while hitting it with a full backswing. I am still working on it. We will see.

Mrs. Jacqueline Kennedy Onassis

Introducing son, John, and daughter, Sue, to Mrs. Onassis at a John F. Kennedy Library Foundation dinner.

CHAPTER 5 | JFK LIBRARY FOUNDATION

JFK LIBRARY FOUNDATION

I was asked to be on the Board and then offered the position of President of the John F. Kennedy Library Foundation by Steve Smith, brother-in-law of John Kennedy. Steve was a very funny guy and someone I liked very much. He was looking to regenerate enthusiasm for the Library, attract new people, etc. This included raising a $20 million endowment. As an entrepreneur who was used to starting with nothing but an idea, I did not view these as challenging tasks given the Kennedy name and power.

However, I was a Kennedy outsider. This was a big asset because I was not beholden to anyone. First I would have to get to know the Kennedy family. I assumed it was very complex, like all families, and I didn't want to create any problems right out of the box. The family would prove to be exceedingly complex. Also, there was a "Kennedy speak." You had to know who was talking about whom in any conversation without hearing the actual name. Since I did not know the Kennedys, I just said to the Foundation staff, "Let's do things the way John Kennedy and Robert Kennedy would have liked them."

Once again, I would learn that the poor are willing to help the poorer. For example, Mark Roosevelt, Director of the Foundation, and Marsha Gomberg created the JFK Library Corps, comprised of kids from poor neighborhoods close to the Library to help other, poorer kids. They were very inspirational. I could tell Mrs. Onassis liked it when they spoke at the annual dinners, which were very much like White House dinners of the Kennedy era, with Isaac Stern as the guest soloist. She told me how very pleased she was with what we were doing. I know other members of the family were, as well.

Also, the Foundation would create incredible opportunities to meet world leaders. Often, Senator Kennedy would be doing political work as part of their visits. I once watched him discussing something with the Prime Minister of Italy with Diddy sitting in between them. Eventually, she got involved in the conversation, and then they listened to her and agreed with what she was saying. I was wondering what she was doing over there, influencing world politics?

Chinook helicopter

The USS John F. Kennedy aircraft carrier we landed on in the Boston Harbor

THE ANNOUNCEMENT

The new JFK Library Foundation announcement was held at the Library with much press and television coverage. It included Senator Kennedy, Caroline Kennedy, and many others. This was my first participation in a Kennedy event, and it was pretty intimidating with all those TV cameras pointed at you, reporters, etc. However, when I spoke right after Caroline, no one was interested in what I had to say in the slightest. As she left the podium, all the cameras and faces swung to follow her, and I ended up talking to myself. The incredible lack of interest in what I had to say literally took my breath away.

If one looked out the Library window, one could see the aircraft carrier, the USS John F. Kennedy, anchored in Boston Harbor. One of its helicopters was located next to the Library to take the Senator and Caroline, etc., to the ship after the event. I

"I spoke right after Caroline, no one was interested in what I had to say in the slightest. As she left the podium, all the cameras and faces swung to follow her, and I ended up talking to myself."

asked Eddie Martin, a long-time aide to Senator Kennedy, if Diddy and I could go along, even though I knew she had a well-known aversion to flying. When Diddy first saw the helicopter, she could not believe that we were going to get on it. With the strong encouragement of Paul Kirk and others, she gamely did. Before liftoff, we had to put on Mae Wests because the Chinook helicopter had open doors and windows, and we were going to be flying over water. I must say that I had some reservations about it myself because the pilot and crew all looked to be about eighteen years old. However, they did a fine job, and landing on a carrier was a unique experience. Funny, but I do not remember how we got off the carrier.

The International Visiting Dignitaries Program of the Library Foundation invited Nelson Mandela to The JFK Library.

NELSON MANDELA

One evening I got a call from Senator Kennedy. He was very excited. Nelson Mandela had just been released from prison in South Africa after 27 years of confinement and was coming to the United States. His first stop was going to be the John F. Kennedy Library. Senator Kennedy was calling me because I was the Chair of The International Visiting Dignitaries Program of the Library Foundation. Nelson Mandela was, by far, the most important visitor the Library ever had. A luncheon for three hundred was scheduled, and I agreed to sponsor it. This meant I would MC it as well.

One unanticipated result of my involvement with this program was that Diddy could get enough of the impossible to get tickets to invite many Black members of her Black & White Boston Coming Together organization to the event. It certainly did not hurt to have an audience with many people of color in it. It was one of the great moments in their lives and ours.

"While he was extremely polite and gracious, he was not in awe of his famous hosts or his surroundings that I could determine."

It intrigued me that Nelson Mandela had such a commanding presence; even though he had just gotten out of jail after 27 years, much of it spent in solitary confinement. While he was extremely polite and gracious, he was not in awe of his famous hosts or his surroundings that I could determine. Having participated in many events at the Library with many important dignitaries, I knew this to be most unusual. I was so struck by it that I could not help but ask Winnie Mandela, who was sitting next to me, how this was the case. How did he have such a calm and confident bearing? My question seemed to come as no surprise to her. Her answer was simple and required no explanation. "He was born to royalty in his tribe in South Africa," she said.

To my great surprise, we passed this billboard on the way home from the event on the Southeast Expressway.

Senator Kennedy, Diddy Cullinane, Caroline Kennedy and John Cullinane

IRISHMAN OF THE YEAR AWARD

The Friends of the John F. Kennedy Library is a group that has been a long-time supporter of the John F. Kennedy Library and really "carries the torch." Each year, they like to single out someone for its Irishman of the Year Award who they feel has been a supporter of the Library in some significant way. One year they selected me.

Diddy prepared a video of family history for the outstanding event. The video also included pictures of Steve Smith, who had since passed on, and Jack Fallon, who was in attendance, seated in a wheelchair. It was a pretty emotional experience for Jack because he was very close to Steve Smith.

"Billy Hutchinson, a Loyalist, and Alex Attwood, a Catholic. They were very effective in their common cause for peace by coming together from different ends of the political spectrum"

At the close of the event, I asked Billy Hutchinson and Alex Attwood to speak extemporaneously. They were two key people from both sides of the divide in Northern Ireland, Billy Hutchinson, a Loyalist, and Alex Attwood, a Catholic. They were very effective in their common cause for peace by coming together from different ends of the political spectrum in Belfast to promote peace in Northern Ireland, a very rare occurrence. They said some nice things about me, but their reaching across the great divide in this way had a huge impact on the audience. Senator Kennedy liked it. John Hume was also at the event, as well, and joined in singing at the end of the evening, "The Town I Love So Well." It was a pretty good night for Northern Ireland and me.

On the way home on the Southeast Expressway, I was shocked to see a massive billboard with my picture on it, congratulating me on the award. It was donated by Ackerley Communications. It was a complete surprise. I almost drove off the road.

Gerard as I knew him.

GERARD DOHERTY

Gerard Doherty, a former recipient of the Irishman of the Year Award, was the event's host. Gerard was an interesting person. He came across as a Boston Irish Catholic politician from Charlestown, which he was. He even cultivated the image that he was from the "wink and nod" school of Boston politics. Still, he was also a Harvard graduate, spoke Russian, was a master political strategist, etc. He also helped everybody he could along the way, particularly those most in trouble, regardless of political party. He also was a big booster of women. As a result, he had loyal friends in the most unlikely places who would do anything for him. He was also a Kennedy confidant and loyalist. I would put him on the Board of my company, along with Bobby Orr, unusual choices at the time, but he fit in perfectly, as did Bobby. I once called him the Bobby Orr of politics.

"He even cultivated the image that he was from the 'wink and nod' school of Boston politics. Still, he was also a Harvard graduate, spoke Russian, was a master political strategist"

As Tom Birmingham, a Rhodes Scholar and former Senate President, said at my event, Gerard often spoke elliptically and that he even said the rosary in code. Gerard seemed to have every politician in Massachusetts speak on my behalf, even if they barely knew me, such as Tom. In fact, I appeared to be incidental to the whole event. I was thinking, "Why is Gerard doing this? What was he up to?" But I knew he operated in mysterious ways.

When he was eighty-nine, Gerard called me saying he had some news that he wanted to tell me. I braced for the worst, but it was not bad news. It was the opposite. He was getting married! He was marrying Regina Quinlan, a long-time friend, sister of the Publisher of this book, a former judge and nun. They had a magnificent wedding in St. Mary's Church in Charlestown, Massachusetts, with a huge turnout, including many VIPs. Everybody was happy for them. It was all very nice.

The Boston Public Library McKim Building in Copley Square

Bill Bulger, Senate President

Bill Taylor, Publisher of *The Boston Globe*

CHAPTER 6 | BPL FOUNDATION

BILL BULGER AND BILL TAYLOR

I received a call from the office of the President of the Massachusetts Senate, William Bulger, to meet him in his office. I was very curious because this was the first time I had such a call. When I entered the Senate President's huge office, someone else was sitting with him. I was shocked to recognize Bill Taylor, Publisher of *The Boston Globe*. I thought *The Boston Globe* and Bulger were arch enemies.

The reason for the meeting was that they wanted me to head up a fundraising effort for the McKim Building of the Boston Public Library. Bill Taylor said he would put the power of *The Boston Globe* behind the effort, a very big commitment. As I headed out the door, he asked, "Could you get Diddy to help?" Eventually, I suggested that we create a Boston Public Library Foundation, and they both agreed.

"I was a high-tech entrepreneur from Route 128, parachuting into a whole new and complex world of Boston social entrepreneurship."

Ironically, no one had told me that the Boston Public Library had undertaken a fundraising effort just a couple of years earlier, and it had failed badly. Nor did they tell me that other organizations felt that they had responsibility for the BPL's fundraising. Nor did they tell me that the Mayor of Boston, Tom Menino, felt that the BPL was his purview and that it was a critical one at that. In other words, I was a high-tech entrepreneur from Route 128, parachuting into a whole new and complex world of Boston social entrepreneurship. It would be a very difficult undertaking. I often said that it would have been easier to form a new company, take it public and just give the Library the money. The good news, though, was that everyone likes libraries, particularly writers. How could we not succeed?

Karyn Wilson, Director of the Boston Public Library Foundation

THE KICKOFF EVENT

The kickoff event for the Boston Public Library Foundation was held at The Algonquin Club, another building designed by Charles Follen McKim, the designer of the magnificent Copley Square Branch of the Boston Public Library. Everyone was there, including Senators Kennedy and Kerry, Governor Weld, and much of the power structure of the City of Boston. Also present was Karyn Wilson, the first Director of the Foundation, who had worked with me at the JFK Library Foundation.

Just prior to the event, I received a call from Jon Barkin, a media consultant, who told me that the BPL had undertaken a fundraising effort a couple of years earlier, but it had collapsed. This is how I learned that there had been one. However, he said he had created the "boards" for a brochure for the effort plus a video that had never been used. He asked if I wanted to take a look at them. They would prove to be beautifully done. It was a bonanza. All we had to do was update a few names, such as changing Mayor Flynn to Mayor Menino, and we had a beautiful brochure. Then,

"The day after the event, I received a letter from the President of the Amelia Peabody Foundation, Mr. Lee, committing $1 million to the McKim Building restoration in Copley Square."

we cut the video from eighteen minutes to nine. Thus, we had all our promotional material done at no cost and available almost immediately. Bill Van Faasen, President of Blue Cross Blue Shield, even agreed to print the brochure for free. We used both the brochure and video at the Kickoff.

The day after the event, I received a letter from the President of the Amelia Peabody Foundation, Mr. Lee, committing $1 million to the McKim Building restoration in Copley Square, our first and significant statement of support.

Richard and Marcia Soden of Boston, Mimi and Jim Segal of Needham, Jackie and Jim Scott of Newton.

PARTY LINES
Photos by Bill Brett

A new chapter for the library

Grandees don't get any grander than the citizens who swept into the main foyer of the McKim Building of the Boston Public Library Thursday to celebrate their own largess toward the restoration of the historic building.

Led by John and Diddy Cullinane of Dedham, they gathered in the polished marble monument on Copley Square for a $1,000-a-person celebration of the ongoing renovation project. Seen were book publisher Nader Darehshori, attorney Jeffrey Rudman, socialite Jacqueline Stepanian, author Carol Goldberg, New England Telephone chief Paul O'Brien, hotelier Robin Brown, newspaper publisher William Taylor, health insurer William Van Faasen (in a red bow tie. "The only way to be loud in the library," he said) and Republican insider Wayne Budd.

And over their lobster and filet dinner, they heard Cullinane say $7.5 million has been raised from

John T. and Diddy Cullinane of Dedham. He's president, she's vice chairwoman of the BPL Foundation.

Dr. Cassandra Simmons and Earl Tate of Boston.

John and Kathryn Hammill of Wellesley. He is president of Fleet Bank.

Connie and Peter Lacaillade of Wellesley

Some publicity from *The Boston Globe* with some good friends from the Boston Public Library Gala

THE GALAS

While I concentrated on fundraising, Diddy focused on the Galas and outreach programs to the Boston schools. For example, Bill Bulger and Bill Taylor agreed to go to Washington, D.C., to meet with the Massachusetts delegation. The Delegation all showed up, and we came back with a commitment of $3 million just for the asking. I put a Foundation Board together made up of many key people you did not see in the social columns, but the BPL had been very important in their lives. Also, I had learned that major corporate givers agree on what level they are going to fund any new effort, so I had to make sure that the BPL was high on their lists.

Diddy did her part by establishing a $1,000 ticket price for the Galas, an unheard-of amount at the time. The Galas would prove to be incredibly successful and lots of fun. For the first one, we put a tent over the McKim building courtyard, which was an experience in itself. Next, we put a tent over Copley Square, and Mayor Menino closed down Dartmouth Street for the event. He once said that he would close down the Central Artery for Diddy.

Everyone was laughing at a Buchwald joke on Diddy, including Mike Wallace.

Diddy used the Gala occasion to position the BPL as the jewel in the crown of all Boston artistic and intellectual organizations by inviting the Board of Trustees of all such organizations to attend. She also arranged, with the help of Paul La Camera and Channel 5, to have the Pops audience attending a concert at Symphony Hall on the evening of the Gala sing Happy Birthday to the Library and show it live on a screen in the tent. She recruited Art Buchwald to host the event, and he brought his good friend Mike Wallace. It was a memorable evening. Everyone had a great time, and the Gala raised $1 million for the Library.

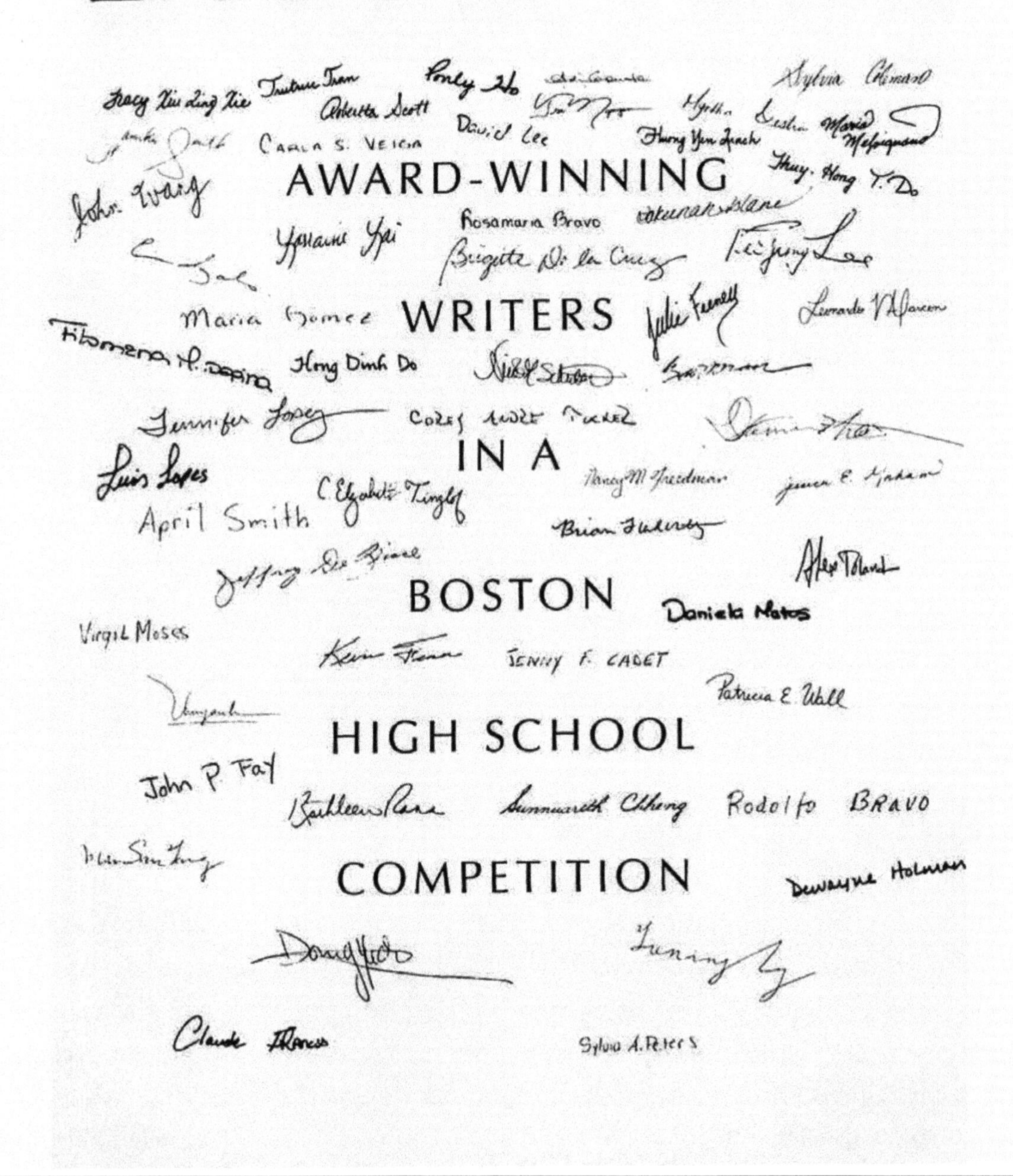

Artwork appeared on two hundred billboards provided by Ackerley Communications.
Book published by Houghton Mifflin.

OUTREACH TO THE BOSTON SCHOOLS

Karyn Wilson had discovered that Ackerley Communications had donated two hundred billboards for the Library's use that were not being used. Diddy set out to create outreach programs for all Boston schools. Rather than hiring professionals to create the ads for the Foundation, Diddy created a design and writing contest to be carried out by the Boston school children celebrating the positive impact of libraries on the community

The winning artwork of the design program would be showcased on billboards near the children's schools, while the successful written work would be published in a book published by Houghton Mifflin, courtesy of Nader Darehshori.

"Diddy set out to create outreach programs for all Boston schools. One included artwork and the other was based on writing skills."

Each year a very special event was held at the JFK Library honoring contest winners and attended by Mayor Menino, teachers involved in the process, a variety of dignitaries and proud family members. Each student received a specific award, a beautifully bound dictionary from Houghton Mifflin, and individual T-shirts with names and photos of Awardees printed on it.

It became a very meaningful and very well attended ceremony for all involved, most of all for the students and their families.

Natalie Jacobson and Chet Curtis hosted the telethon.

THE TELETHON

I called Jim Coppersmith, head of Channel 5, about a possible telethon for the Boston Public Library. He was negative. He said they do not work. They had to be about kids. I said the Library was all about kids. He said, ok, but it costs $100,000.

Not long afterward, at a Parkman House function, Bill Van Faasen, of Blue Cross and Blue Shield, agreed to provide the funding and staffing – the deal was done!

The result would be one of the most outstanding promotional videos I have ever seen, *The Boston Public Library - It Speaks Volumes.* I suspect Paul La Camera, General Manager of Channel 5 and a big fan of the Library, went full out with Chet Curtis and Natalie Jacobson hosting it.

"Chet and Natalie were interviewing famous authors such as David McCullough, John Updike, Robert Parker, and others such as Ted Kennedy, and many more about the importance of the Library."

Jim Coppersmith said it was the only telethon ever where the viewership was higher at the end than at the beginning. Chet and Natalie were interviewing famous authors such as David McCullough, John Updike, Robert Parker, and others such as Ted Kennedy, and many more about the importance of the Library to them. It raised $140,000. A major portion of it came from The Birmingham Foundation, courtesy of Paul Birmingham.

Everyone seemed to love being part of it, including the Channel 5 and Blue Cross people and the BPL staff. They were doing good work. As I said before, everyone likes libraries. The video still exits. If I were the BPL fundraisers, I would use it almost exactly as it is but just add some new authors and VIPs, etc. The video was hugely successful from a public relations point of view because it showcased some of the Library's great staff, like Sinclair Hitchings, Curator of Prints, and some of its wonderful treasures and services that most people had never seen or heard of before. This work is now being carried on by the Boston Public Library Fund.

Bill Bulger talking to President GHWB or WJC and breaking up Elaine Kamarck and John Kerry

Bill Bulger is breaking up Diddy

CHAPTER 7 | POLITICAL

POLITICAL

Politics has always interested me because politicians seem to have so much fun. They certainly did in Boston. They did not talk about issues. They sang, they told jokes, recited poetry, and did the business of politics on the side with a wink or a nod. Boston was unique in this regard.

Bill Bulger led the way with his St. Patrick's Day breakfasts. However, they were all good at it, not just Bulger. This included the Kennedys, Tip O'Neill, Bill Weld, Governor Sargent, and many others such as George Keverian, Billy Sutton, and a host of characters. Then, there were legendary people such as James Michael Curley.

"The good guys were often the bad guys. It seems that politics in Massachusetts is 12 layers deep, with lots of history and grudges."

However, listening to them discussing some story of the day in the paper, the real story was always different. The good guys were often the bad guys. It seems that politics in Massachusetts is 12 layers deep, with lots of history and grudges. It is tough to know who's doing what to whom and why. I consider myself knowledgeable, and I can only get down to six layers.

I have found, though, that most politicians are much smarter than most people think, they care about helping people, and they work very hard at it. When they run for office they put everything on the line, and when they lose everybody knows it, and it is over, literally, overnight. That is why I call them the ultimate entrepreneurs.

Chancellor Helmut Kohl, Hillary Rodham Clinton, and President Clinton

DINNER AT THE WHITE HOUSE

I had Chaired the New England Business Executives for Clinton/Gore and was very involved in promoting Clinton's peace agenda via jobs in Northern Ireland. I mentioned to Al From, President of the Democratic Leadership Council, that I thought it was odd I had never been invited to the Clinton White House, given my support for the above.

Not long after, Diddy and I received a fancy invitation to attend a White House dinner for Chancellor Helmut Kohl of Germany. I was amazed to be seated at President Clinton's table. What turned out to be very valuable was that I was able to talk to the President about an idea I had for creating jobs in Northern Ireland

"Diddy was at another table close by, seated with Tony Bennett, the evening's performer. I would wave at her, and Tony would wave back, thinking I was waving at him."

based on an Israeli/American program called BIRD (Israel-U.S. Binational Industrial Research and Development Foundation). He knew all about BIRD, the only one I discussed it with who did. He gave me a card with his fax number and assistant's name, Nancy Hernreich, so I could send him material, which I did, and he always responded.

Diddy was at another table close by, seated with Tony Bennett, the evening's performer. I would wave at her, and Tony would wave back, thinking I was waving at him. After dinner, we were a little late for seating for Bennett's performance, and we were ushered down the center aisle to seats in the front row right next to the Clintons, the Gores, and the guest of honor Chancellor Helmut Kohl. We were just in time for their arrival. Sitting there, I could feel curious eyes on us from all these powerful people, such as Henry Kissinger, seated just to my right. I knew what he, and others, were thinking. "Who are these people, and what are they doing there?"

Diddy and I receiving the Senator Paul Tsongas Award at the Massachusetts Democratic Party State Dinner

A POLITICAL CAREER SNUFFED OUT

Diddy and I were selected to receive the Senator Paul Tsongas Award at the Massachusetts Democratic Party State Dinner. As you may note, I have a tuxedo on, the only one in the room. So, right away, I am off to a bad start. I gave a forgettable speech that I had labored over for months, and then it was Diddy's turn to speak. Ted Kennedy had come to introduce me, but nobody had told him that Diddy would speak, too, until I did. She had written her remarks on the back of an envelope during the car ride in. It was about her good friend, Johanna Schonmetzler, who had recently settled in the United States with her husband, anesthesiologist Dr. Heinz Schonmetzler, and what our democracy meant to her.

"She had written her remarks on the back of an envelope during the car ride in. It was about her good friend, Johanna Schonmetzler, who had recently settled in the United States with her husband, anesthesiologist Dr. Heinz Schonmetzler, and what our democracy meant to her."

She had recently attended an outdoor rally on Boston Common for a Walter Mondale event and was impressed by the variety of people streaming out of offices, etc., people of a wide variety of backgrounds, financial, ethnic, racial, coming to witness an aspiring candidate for high national office.

This was the America Johanna had always envisioned! Addressing this Democratic Party audience, Diddy reminded them that these were the people the Party should always represent!

Diddy got a standing ovation. My political career was over, if there ever was going to be one. I could tell because, afterward, when I ran into Congressman Chet Atkins who was responsible for the dinner, he said, with great enthusiasm, "You were good, but Diddy was great!" This was the kiss of death.

Speaking of kisses, I got a big kick out of all those on the dais who tried to kiss Diddy on the cheek as she passed by. Little did they know how fast she could move, but I did. They kept missing and were kissing air.

Later, I was asked to run for Lt. Governor by a famous politician who was running for Governor, but I politely declined.

Peter Lynch, Tip O'Neill, and my St Augustine's Episcopalian shirt.

Friends Tom Swan, John Cunningham, and Bobby Orr at the golf dinner

SPEAKER TIP O'NEILL

We arranged for an annual golf tournament and dinner at Eastward Ho! Golf Club in Chatham and invited all the CEOs in the Greater Boston business community I knew just to have a good time and use up my house minimum fees. Eastward Ho! is a beautiful course surrounded by water that everyone likes to play. Nothing CEOs like better than to be invited to play golf with their peers. Lots of business done on the side. Some would even fly their planes into Chatham airport to attend.

The big attraction would be Tip O'Neill holding forth afterward at dinner with Washington inside baseball and humor. Many Republican attendees thought Tip was just a big Boston Irish Pol, but they learned otherwise. They would come away very impressed. I did not think that Tip would make the last dinner we had because his health was failing badly. He came, played nine holes, drove himself home and was back in time for dinner, holding forth as usual with great humor. That was the last time we played the tournament. Without Tip, it would never be the same.

"The big attraction would be Tip O'Neill holding forth afterward at dinner with Washington inside baseball and humor."

Every year Diddy and I would have a big summer party for the neighbors with a sing-along at our place in Chatham, and we would make sure Tip could make it. One year, Tip came along with Ted Kennedy, Joe Moakley, and Bill Bulger. They were all gathered around the piano, singing. Our local real estate agent was on the other side of the piano, looking at them wide-eyed. From where he came from, politically, these were the politicians he had been warned about his whole life. They were the enemy, and here they were in Chatham, standing right across from him! He was fuming and sweating and kept requesting that they sing, "God Bless America." Finally, they did. This seemed to make him feel much better, and he began to relax. Maybe, they weren't Commies after all.

SAM J. ERVIN, JR., N.C., CHAIRMAN
HOWARD H. BAKER, JR., TENN. VICE CHAIRMAN
HERMAN E. TALMADGE, GA. — EDWARD J. GURNEY, FLA.
DANIEL K. INOUYE, HAWAII — LOWELL P. WEICKER, JR., CONN.
JOSEPH M. MONTOYA, N. MEX.

SAMUEL DASH
CHIEF COUNSEL AND STAFF DIRECTOR
FRED D. THOMPSON
MINORITY COUNSEL
RUFUS L. EDMISTEN
DEPUTY COUNSEL

United States Senate

SELECT COMMITTEE ON
PRESIDENTIAL CAMPAIGN ACTIVITIES
(PURSUANT TO S. RES. 60, 93D CONGRESS)
WASHINGTON, D.C. 20510

January 31, 1974

Mr. John Cullinane, President
Cullinane Corporation
One Boston Place
Boston, Massachusetts 02108

Dear Mr. Cullinane:

As Chairman of the United States Senate Select Committee on Presidential Campaign Activities, I want to express my appreciation for the use of the soft ware package developed by Cullinane Corporation and the assistance provided by you and members of your staff. I was informed that the system performed satisfactorily, and reduced the man hours needed for program writing.

You know, John, a man can always take pride from an act of serving his country in the way that he knows best; your actions reflect favorably upon you as a man, and as a citizen interested in the welfare of this country.

I, and the other members of the Committee, appreciate the interest you have taken in the activities of this Committee and the contribution that you have made.

Sincerely,

Sam J. Ervin, Jr.

Sam J. Ervin, Jr.
Chairman

I received this letter from Senator Sam Ervin, Jr., Chairman of the Select Committee on Presidential Campaign Activities. It was arranged by Sam Dash, Chief Counsel of the Committee.

WATERGATE

A couple of years ago, I was at the Democratic National Committee office in Washington, D.C. After the meeting, they took me down to the basement and showed me a file cabinet. I had no idea why they were showing it to me. Then, they told me that it was the actual cabinet that the Watergate burglars were trying to break into when they got caught. I was astounded. I did not know that the file cabinet still existed. Behind the cabinet is the front page of *The Washington Post* and the first coverage regarding the break-in. Little did they know that I was involved, tangentially, in the original Watergate Hearings. I received this letter (opposite page) from Senator Sam Ervin, Jr., Chairman of the Select Committee on Presidential Campaign Activities. It was arranged by Sam Dash, Chief Counsel of the Committee, for the use of my company's software product in computer tape analysis.

The Watergate file cabinet that the burglars were trying to break into.

Meeting President Reagan at The White House.

PRESIDENT RONALD REAGAN

Dee d'Arbeloff, President of Millipore Corporation, helped create the American Business Conference, which was made up of young, fast-growing, entrepreneurial companies like mine. Jack Albertine, highly regarded around Washington, was recruited to run it. Dee asked me to join. As a result, I would go to Washington, D.C., for the first time and meet with politicians like Senator Paul Tsongas and learn some things. One was that our companies were paying taxes at the 34% rate, and the big companies were paying at a 24% rate. I chalked this up to lobbyists. We did not have any, and they had a lot. Also, I was surprised at how unsophisticated many of the CEOs were about politics. Some thought that they could tell these politicians what to do and they should do it, irrespective of the merits of their cases.

"I did meet President Reagan twice. The first was at The White House with other members of the American Business Conference, and he made his famous comment about taxes, which was, "Make my day."

I did meet President Reagan twice. The first was at The White House with other members of the American Business Conference, and he made his famous comment about taxes, which was, "Make my day." The second was at an event hosted by Dee at his company in association with the Mass High Tech Council. As a fellow Council member, I was asked to participate in a roundtable that would ask President Reagan questions, which were assigned, while a much larger group of CEOs looked on. It was also televised.

President Reagan was late because they made an impromptu stop at the Eire Pub in Dorchester for a photo op. However, this allowed me to talk at length with another CEO seated next to me. He was very conservative and from the South. However, the more we talked, the more we agreed on everything. Yet, politically, we were at opposite ends of the spectrum. Strange.

I gave the book to somebody in this room.

BOOK

On another visit to The White House to meet President Clinton, I brought a book with me that I thought he might like, *How the Irish Saved Civilization*, by Thomas Cahill. I purposefully kept the book's cover face down so he could not see it. I wondered how curious he would be. He spent the whole hour glancing at the book. After the meeting, I gave it to a staff person and wondered what happened to it.

"How the Irish Saved Civilization, by Thomas Cahill. I purposefully kept the book's cover face down so he could not see it. I wondered how curious he would be."

Sometime later, I had a meeting with Senator Reed of Rhode Island, and we were discussing Clinton and his love of books. Senator Reed told me that he was on Air Force 1 with President Clinton while coming back from a trip to Bosnia. It was 3:00 a.m. when Clinton came bounding down the aisle full of enthusiasm, wanting to talk about this book he had just read. They all groaned because they wanted to sleep. The book was, *How the Irish Saved Civilization.*

During the visit to The White House, someone photographed me shaking hands with President Clinton (photo at left). It was not an official photograph. Anyway, the photo appeared on CNN, etc., and was shown worldwide as part of a story on fundraising at The White House.

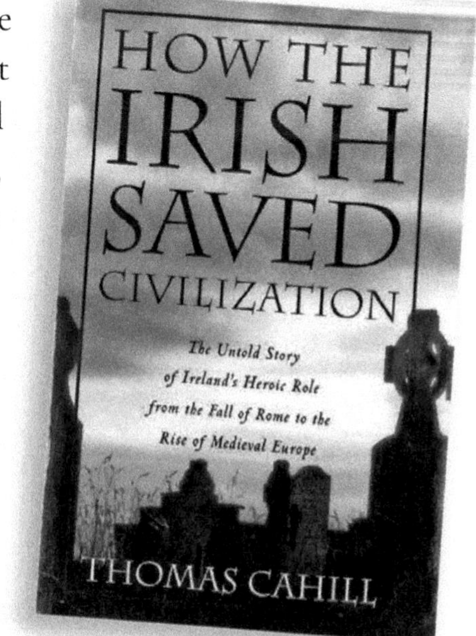

Typical air traffic control tower.

FEDERAL AVIATION ADMINISTRATION (FAA)

In his last days in office, President Clinton appointed me to a new oversight committee of the Federal Aviation Administration (FAA) responsible for America's Air Traffic Control system.

The swearing-in session took place in an auditorium separate from The White House. When President Clinton was at the podium, I was sitting directly behind him and could see the audience clearly. There were about 200 men and about 100 women staring at us. I immediately noticed that all the 100 women were smiling and gazing with great affection toward President Clinton. On the other hand, not one of the 200 men was. I can only speculate why this was the case. The bottom line, I believe, is that women liked Clinton. Men did, too, but not entirely with the same enthusiasm.

"Airlines often use less experienced pilots on weekends and set minimums of 400 feet, whereas more experienced pilots can land at 300 feet."

Sometime later, on my way home from a trip to Ireland, I asked the stewardess on Aer Lingus if the pilot would let me come into the cabin, watch them fly the plane, and ask questions in my new role. The pilot agreed. There was not much to see, though. The plane flew itself across the Atlantic as the pilot pushed a button every so often. However, he did say all he needed to land was 200 feet, and he had never been routed to another airport because of weather conditions. This was encouraging.

I also visited the Logan Airport Control Tower one Saturday morning when there was very bad fog and low visibility. I noticed that little Cape Air flights from the Islands were landing, but a United jet from Cleveland aborted. I heard the Air Traffic Controller mutter, "Weekend Warrior." I asked him what that meant. He said airlines often use less experienced pilots on weekends and set minimums of 400 feet, whereas more experienced pilots can land at 300 feet. I doubt those passengers on the aborted United flight were aware of this.

Know Your
POWER
A Message to America's Daughters
Nancy Pelosi
with
Amy Hill Hearth

NANCY PELOSI, MESSAGING

Congressman Ed Markey came to my office one day with the Leader of the House, Nancy Pelosi. In conversation, she mentioned that her number one problem was messaging. I told her that I knew how to do that. I had created a process for producing good sales messages at my company. Otherwise, we would have gone out of business because I learned that it was impossible to get an agreement on any message without it. She asked me if I would come to Washington, D.C., and help her create one.

When I went to Washington, I anticipated meeting with a few aides in a small conference room. When Congressman Markey and his Chief of Staff opened the door, there were about 15 Congressmen and women, many famous such as Congressman Clyburn, and about 30 staff members sitting there. I was stunned. I had never conducted a messaging session with such a large group before. However, after we completed the session, everyone burst into applause. They knew what I was doing was making something look easy that they struggled with all the time. It is getting the agreement that is the challenging part.

However, in 2006 the Democrats won back the House with the "6for06" message, which was the six pieces of legislation they would pass in the first 100 hours that they controlled the House, and they did. In other words, the Democrats had a plan that addressed the six key concerns of the American people. As such, they were the only political party that did. Also, the winds were blowing in the Democrats' favor. Nancy Pelosi discussed this in her book, *Know Your Power.*

This is the event after which we created the Irish message for Biden. Diddy on the left and Linda Dorcena Forry (in the background) helped create it.

JOE BIDEN, MESSAGING

When Joe Biden was running for Vice President, he attended a luncheon for a group of Irish Americans put together by Ed Forry, Publisher of *The Boston Irish Reporter*. In his remarks, he said he needed an outreach message to sell Obama to Irish Americans. So, we decided to stay after lunch and create one with my message process and have it for him before we left, and we did.

At the time, I was head of outreach to the Irish American community for the Obama/Biden campaign in New England. One Sunday morning, I was at the Irish Cultural Centre (ICC) in Canton, Massachusetts, looking it over for a possible fundraiser site.

As serendipity would have it, a large group was having brunch at the ICC after attending Mass. The Manager asked if I would like to address the crowd on behalf of Obama right then. I was very apprehensive. I had never given a political speech before, and this may not be too friendly a group, given some issues. Also, what was I going to say? Then, I thought of the message we had recently created for Biden. The message was that "Obama was the only candidate that addressed the six key interests of Irish Americans. He was smart, well educated, walked in our shoes, was a man of faith, and experience." When I got to the sixth point where I said, "and Obama has Irish roots," I could hear murmuring across the room. I knew what they were saying, "Obama has Irish roots? I did not know that!" Very few people did at the time. My speech took about three minutes. I do not know how many friends I made for Obama, but I know I made some, and I neutralized others. I said that Obama was the only candidate who addressed their key concerns and what they were. What is wrong with that? It is a good sales message.

Then Joe Kennedy, who was doing outreach for the Obama/Biden campaign in New Hampshire, heard about it and asked me to help him create messages for the Latino, French American, and Greek Americans. He put together focus groups, and we created all three messages on a Thursday morning. He was using them that weekend.

Longworth House Office Building, Washington, D.C.

THE CHANGING OF THE OFFICES

When the Democrats won the House, Nancy Pelosi invited me to speak to the House Democratic Caucus on messaging in January of 2006, just before they took over control of the House. As I walked down the hallways of the Longworth House Office Building, I was amazed to see furniture piled high in the middle of the massive corridors of the building, including electronics, telephone systems, etc. This was the case on each floor. All the offices were empty. As someone familiar with moving, this was a massive moving job with just days to go. What was going on?

> *"When one party loses control of the House, the members of the losing party have to move out of their choice offices with their great views of the Capitol, etc., to the basement or back offices."*

When one party loses control of the House, the members of the losing party have to move out of their choice offices with their great views of the Capitol, etc., to the basement or back offices. In this case, it was the Republicans. The Democrats, in turn, were moving back from oblivion to the choice offices. It is the most dramatic example of the transfer of power in our Democracy that I can imagine. Congressmen and women just hate to lose those nice offices with incredible views because it signifies that they are out of power until they, once again, regain control of the House. In Washington, when you have been voted out of power, you are really out of power. It is no fun.

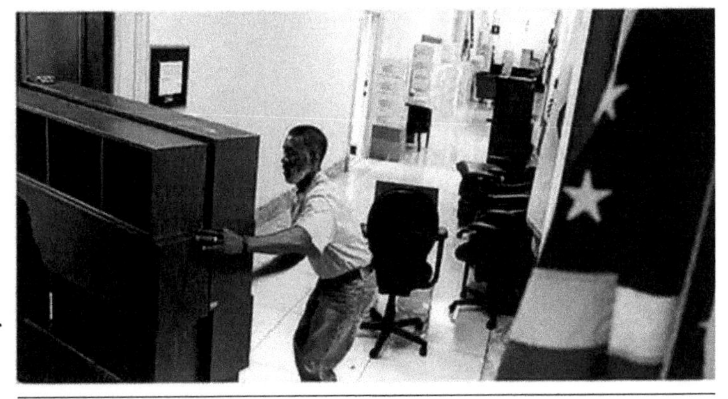

Moving day at the Longworth House Office Building

Richard Cavanagh, former Executive Dean of the Kennedy School and good friend.

CHAPTER 8 | KENNEDY SCHOOL

KENNEDY SCHOOL

When I sold my company, I was looking for something new to do. I had always been intrigued by how the dials of government get turned. It all starts with an idea. Many ideas originate at Harvard's Kennedy School. So, when Richard Cavanagh, Executive Dean, and University Professor John Dunlop offered me the chance to become a Senior Fellow at the Center for Business & Government of The Kennedy School, I was more than happy to accept it.

I had known Richard Cavanagh since he was with McKinsey & Co., and he had included my company in his best-selling book, "The Winning Performance." Richard has a remarkable Irish heritage with family members who were involved in the creation of the Irish Free State. He would be enormously helpful and supportive of peace in Northern Ireland. This included enabling Frank Costello to bring many of the 450 cross-community "Leaders of Tomorrow" to the Kennedy School. This was hugely important because many of these attendees are in important positions today in the Republic and Northern Ireland. Richard even arranged for me to represent Harvard in *The Irish Times* debate celebrating Trinity College's 400th anniversary. They wanted someone with an Irish background, and I fit the bill.

Professor Dunlop was in his nineties but still going strong. He believed that where government and business converged, important things happen. I believe he was right. He advised me, "Do something, don't waste your time here." So, I wrote a book, "Entrepreneur's Survival Guide - 101 Tips for Managing in Good Times and Bad," and a paper, "Widows and Orphans," which was a walk down Wall Street from the perspective of an entrepreneur. I would also organize seminars on critical issues of the day for CEOs and later participate in two Private/Public Partnership seminars, one with Frank Costello on Northern Ireland and another discussing Black & White economic issues in Boston. I am still involved as a member of the Advisory Council of the now named Mossavar-Rahmani Center for Business and Government, chaired by Professor Larry Summers and John Haigh.

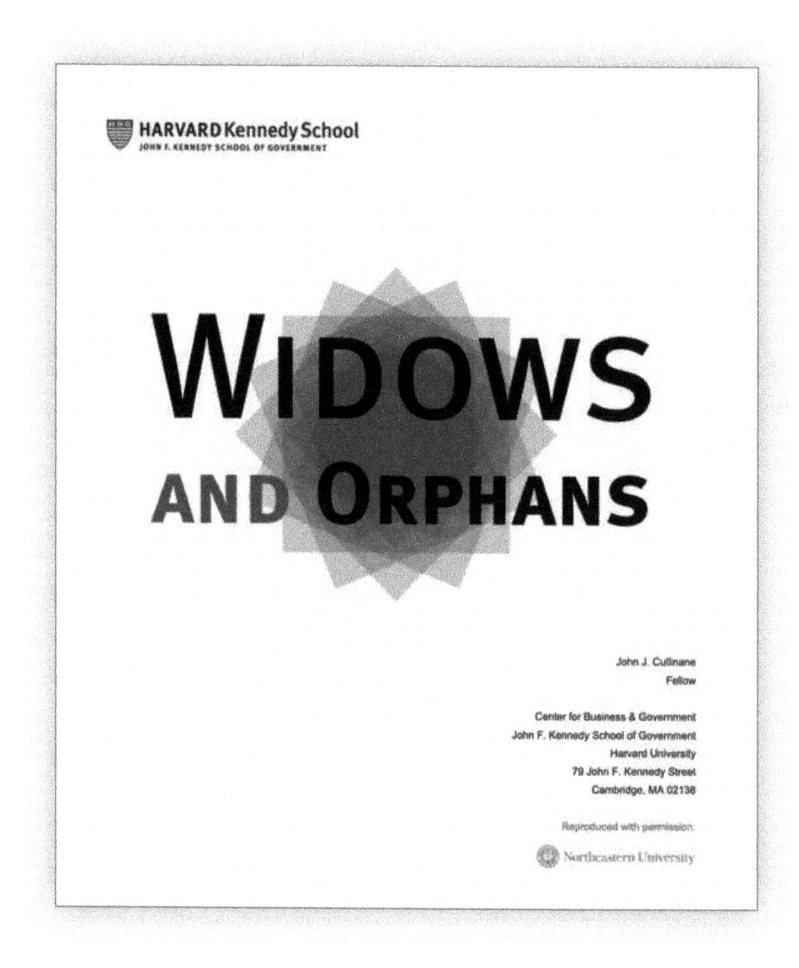

HARVARD Kennedy School
JOHN F. KENNEDY SCHOOL OF GOVERNMENT

WIDOWS AND ORPHANS

John J. Cullinane
Fellow

Center for Business & Government
John F. Kennedy School of Government
Harvard University
79 John F. Kennedy Street
Cambridge, MA 02138

Northeastern University

WIDOWS AND ORPHANS

After much trepidation, I turned in my paper, "Widows and Orphans," for Professor Dunlop to read. Remember, this is Harvard, and he is a University Professor. He told me it read "like a Canterbury Tale." I did not know what he meant, so I asked my son, John Jr., who was an English major at Harvard. My son said, "Difficult to understand, but there was a message in it." For one thing, I had forecasted the demise of the American automobile industry because the Japanese put customer satisfaction first, whereas American companies put it way down the list. It would be just a matter of time before they went bankrupt, and they did.

"In other words, investment banks, which I call 'speculation banks,' were not allowed to sell risky securities to unsophisticated buyers"

Tom Stemberg, the founder of Staples, said it was the best paper he had ever read. However, in writing it, I was curious about how Wall Street came to be, particularly the Securities Act of 1933. When I asked around, I was told I should see Professor Ray Vernon. When I knocked on his door, I said, "I am told you know something about the Securities Act of 1933." "Yes," he replied casually, "I wrote it." I almost fell over. Such is Harvard, I would learn.

Subsequently, I met with Harvard Business School Professor Joe Auerbach, who was also around during the great Wall Street Crash of 1929. He said people were furious at the banks for selling them the worthless securities that led to The Crash.

Wall Street did the same thing with unregulated derivatives not long ago. They never learn. The Securities Act of 1933 put the onus on the seller of stocks, not the buyer. In other words, investment banks, which I call "speculation banks," were not allowed to sell risky securities to unsophisticated buyers such as "Widows and Orphans," hence the name of my paper.

Professor Ray Vernon

PROFESSOR RAY VERNON

Professor Ray Vernon was a renowned scholar who played a key role in the creation of the SEC. He was also heavily involved in creating The Marshall Plan and the International Monetary Fund (IMF). Later he would be referred to as the "Father of Globalization."

Professor Vernon was also a very nice and helpful person. He once told me an incredible story about his brother. He did not tell me his name that I can remember. However, he said that his brother did the Bataan Death March twice, the only one ever to do so. The first trip was as a doctor in an ambulance carrying those not capable of walking. When he returned to get more, the Japanese made him give up the ambulance and walk the route. He then was put on a freighter destined for a

"He was also heavily involved in creating The Marshall Plan and the International Monetary Fund (IMF). Later he would be referred to as the Father of Globalization."

prison camp in Japan which was torpedoed. He was very fortunate that he managed to surface with a couple of others, plus a big box, before the ship went down. When they were able to open the box, it contained a sailboat which they put together and sailed to China. When he reached China, the Japanese captured him again and sent him to a prisoner of war camp in Japan.

Years passed when there was a rumor that something big had happened in some nearby city. Then, all the Japanese guards just disappeared. So, he just walked out the camp gate, and no one stopped him. He walked to Nagasaki or Hiroshima, I cannot remember which one, observed the nuclear bomb destruction, and learned that the war was over. He walked to a port where there were American ships, including a destroyer. He decided to take the destroyer home to America, even though it was slower, because it had a lot of medical journals on it that he could read.

I told Professor Vernon that he should have someone write up this incredible story for posterity, and I knew someone who would do it. He demurred, so I am pleased to be able to do it in his memory. I hope my memory is accurate.

From a seminar on Northern Ireland with Frank Costello regarding initiatives that we were personally involved in.

ALEX ATTWOOD AND BILLY HUTCHINSON

Alex Attwood and Billy Hutchinson came to Boston from Belfast to run the Boston Marathon together. This was a very significant thing to happen because Billy was a Loyalist and a member of the Progressive Unionist Party, and Alex was a Nationalist and a member of John Hume's SDLP Party. It was a very rare cross-community initiative. One reason is that Billy had been in prison for 17 years for killing two innocent Catholics as a 17-year-old. He would spend his time in prison getting an education and became a community leader when he was released.

"Billy was a Loyalist and a member of the Progressive Unionist Party, and Alex was a Nationalist and a member of John Hume's SDLP Party. It was a very rare cross-community initiative."

As a Fellow at The Center for Business and Government at The Kennedy School, I thought it would be good if Alex and Billy were showcased in an event at the Forum. However, when I broached the subject with the person who headed the Forum, she was not very enthusiastic. When they had Irish events in the past, she said few Irish showed up. I said the reason was probably that few Irish names were on the invitation list. She said she would do the event if I could guarantee attendance.

With Frank Costello's help, it was no problem at all. We had standing room only for both the forum and the dinner. Professor Louise Richardson, Kennedy School academic on terrorism, was the moderator. The session had a significant impact on the audience. Later, Diddy and I would host Billy and Alex at an event at our home, and they would also speak at the Irishman of the Year event at the JFK Library. More recently, Frank Costello and I conducted a session on Public-Private Partnerships in the Northern Ireland Peace Process because everything we did seemed to be a public/private partnership. Ironically, Professor Dunlop had encouraged me to do this years before, but it finally happened when Scott Leland, of the Mossavar-Rahmani Center for Business and Government, arranged it to a good turnout.

M.L. Carr and Governor Weld, attendees at the Economic Conference.

BLACK & WHITE ECONOMIC CONFERENCE

With Dean Richard Cavanagh's support, a Black & White Conference was held at the Kennedy School. Its focus was on how Black-owned businesses could get better access to White-controlled companies, a huge problem even today. It attracted 200 participants from both communities. They included Senator John Kerry and Governor Weld, plus business types such as Paul Fireman, Reebok, Paul O'Brien, NET&T and Bill Van Faasen, Blue Cross Blue Shield. Members of the Black community included M.L. Carr, Boston Celtics, Ron Homer, Boston Bank of Commerce, James Miller, AB&W, Inc, Bernard West, Urban Underwriters, and others.

"From this meeting evolved the Black & White on Green Golf Tournament run by Diddy that proved so effective in promoting social interaction between groups."

From this meeting evolved the Black & White on Green Golf Tournament run by Diddy that proved so effective in promoting social interaction between groups. It was decided to have it at Franklin Park Golf Course, where few Boston CEOs had ever played before. They were surprised to find it an excellent course that Mayor Menino and Parks Commissioner Justine Liff were completely renovating, including a new clubhouse. Bill Van Faasen would be the first Chair of the tournament and named it *Black & White on Green.*

Dunmore East looks amazingly like Chatham, Massachusetts. It is referred to as the sunny southeast of Ireland and, like Chatham, has many tourists, restaurants, beaches, etc.

CHAPTER 9 | IRELAND

IRELAND

My parents and all my relatives were from Ireland. Yet, I never knew much about Ireland or even inquired about their experiences. I was an American of Irish descent more interested in playing baseball, etc. I had no interest in taking Irish dancing classes like my cousins. How did I know that there would be something like Riverdance someday? I could have done that.

I once asked my mother what her trip over on the boat was like, assuming it must have been bad. "Oh no," she said. "It was fun. We had music and dancing." I do remember that my aunt, Margaret Mulcahy, would always sing "Danny Boy" at any family event. She must have been quite the entrepreneur because she owned a rooming house in Harvard Square and five houses in Arlington. She lost all but one in The Great Depression.

When I finally visited the place of my mother's birth in Dunmore East, County Waterford, I went looking for someone who might know her. I knocked on one door, and the fellow who came out said he was just a summer visitor. "Maybe, you should try Mr. O'Neill next door," he said. "He's been here a long time." When Mr. O'Neill answered the door, he looked like the long-lost twin brother of Tip O'Neill. I asked him if he knew my mother, Margaret Cullinane. He said he did not. Then I said her maiden name was Margaret Fitzgerald. His eyes lit up. "Oh, Maggie Fitzgerald! I knew her well. I used to dance with her all the time!" Then he added, "She was older than me, though." This made me smile because he was about ninety.

Dunmore East looks amazingly like Chatham, Massachusetts. It is referred to as the sunny southeast of Ireland and, like Chatham, has many tourists, restaurants, beaches, etc. It even has a fishing fleet with boats similar in size and numbers to those in Chatham that catch the same fish. Dunmore East's fishermen recently stood up to the Russian navy, and the Russians backed down from conducting exercises over their fishing grounds. As a result, Irish fishermen became famous worldwide, and Chatham would like to start a port-to-port relationship with them.

Signing an agreement in Ireland with Governor Weld, Barry Murphy, Joyce Plotkin and Irish Officials on the Trade Mission.

BARRY MURPHY

Barry Murphy headed up Forbairt, the Irish agency handling the Irish indigenous software industry. He used to visit me from time to time, trying to get me to go to Ireland. Finally, I relented and agreed to go. I was not expecting much when he arranged for me to meet with 21 Irish software entrepreneurs. However, I would be very impressed. They were all doing advanced work, but below the radar. No one knew they existed, though, and no venture capital money was available to them. Then, he had me meet with the Presidents of three Irish universities. I was equally impressed.

"I came away with a new appreciation of Ireland as a country of intellectualism with a great focus on education."

I came away with a new appreciation of Ireland as a country of intellectualism with a great focus on education. It was only a matter of time before some software companies would emerge and become very successful. Iona Technologies was the first.

However, in Ireland, there was an anti-entrepreneurship mentality at the time. If you failed at something, it could be held against you for generations. So, I decided to promote these Irish software companies in the United States with Barry's help. Others included Jim O'Brien, UMASS, the New England/Israeli Chamber of Commerce, etc. We held conferences at the Harvard Business School and the JFK Library showcasing ten companies from Ireland, Northern Ireland, and Israel for American audiences of venture capitalists, etc. The Irish CEOs were remarkably gifted in presenting their companies. They certainly were articulate or, as my mother called it, "The Gift of Gab."

Also, I asked Barry to go to Israel and write a report on "Israel, a High-Tech Role Model for the Island of Ireland." It was well-received in Irish government circles.

Barry also had a beautiful singing voice. He sang the Irish National Anthem in English at Croke Park before an American football game. I had never heard it sung in English before or since. It is a beautiful song in English. The people around us were most impressed.

Our first stop in Ireland was with Barry at The Phoenix House to sign agreements between Joyce Plotkin, President of the Massachusetts Software Council, and its Irish equivalent.

Alasdair McDonnell, Frank Costello, Lord Mayor Hugh Smyth, Mayor Menino, John Cullinane, and John Cullinane, Jr. Mayor Menino was a huge supporter of peace in Northern Ireland.

CHAPTER 10 | NORTHERN IRELAND

FRANK COSTELLO

I never expected to be in Belfast, Northern Ireland, in my life. That all changed when I received a call from Frank Costello late one afternoon.

Frank was the former Chief of Staff for Congressman Joe Kennedy, a consultant based in Belfast who had substantial contacts in the Republic of Ireland and a Ph.D. in Irish history.

He asked me to meet with a cross-community group that was interested in jobs, the only topic that would bring these leaders into the same room. Both poor communities, Loyalist and Catholic, were suffering from 60% unemployment rates. The most violence took place in these communities.

As serendipity would have it, The Ireland Fund was having its big annual Boston dinner two weeks later. On the spur of the moment, I invited the group to join Diddy and me at our table at the event. They jumped at the opportunity, a good sign.

I received a call the next day to ask me if I would Chair a State Trade Mission to Dublin. The day after Belfast was added. Two days earlier I never thought I would be in Belfast in my life, now I was going. I would go another fourteen times.

I was also asked to recruit CEOs to go on the trip, with a focus on finance and IT companies and the Ireland Fund Dinner was the perfect place to do it. The Belfast group arrived for the dinner and, thanks to Frank Costello, brought with them Lord Mayor Hugh Smyth, a member of the Progressive Unionist Party, a Loyalist. While at the dinner, I was introduced to Ted Kelly President of Liberty Mutual who, amazingly, was from Belfast. I told him that I had a table full of people from Belfast, including the Lord Mayor and asked him if he would like to meet them. He was, obviously, very surprised. Ted had not been back to Belfast for 25 years. His family home and business had been burned out by the Loyalists. This chance meeting would lead Liberty Mutual to open an especially important facility in Belfast with eight hundred jobs. He announced this at the second Clinton Trade and Investment Conference held in Pittsburg. This would lead to other companies making major job creating commitments to Belfast. Frank's call was certainly paying dividends for Belfast.

John Cullinane being interviewed at one of Frank Costello's many stops.

THE TRADE MISSION

My first glimpse of Belfast was a city with nothing new in thirty years. Few shops were open, and no new buildings to be seen but a lot of barbed wire. We stayed at the Europa Hotel, the most bombed hotel in Europe. A big explosion in the middle of the night woke up John, Jr., and me causing some anxiety. Strangely, in the morning, no one seemed to know anything about it or even heard it. Frank said that was the way it was. John, Jr., was working for Mayor Menino at the time, and that is why he was on the trip as his representative. Mayor Menino was a huge supporter of peace in Northern Ireland and did many things to help it.

Frank Costello arranged my schedule since Governor Weld had his schedule that often did not include me, even though I was Chair of the Trade Mission. This would prove to be fortuitous because Frank knew everyone on all sides of the conflict and was highly regarded by them, as well as by the media. As a result, I met all kinds of people who would never be on the Governor's agenda, such as the wonderful students at Meánscoil, an Irish language school. One by-product was that Frank's events were covered by his friends in the media so that when we got back to the hotel, they were the ones on the six o'clock news. I was even on Belfast's most popular radio news station in the morning. I think there was some grumbling on the part of some of the Governor's staff about this. I wondered what all those cameras and lights were doing at some of our stops.

As a former Chief of Staff to Congressman Joe Kennedy, Frank did not miss a beat. I was even receiving some awards. However, it was a challenge and hard work because Frank had me scheduled every hour with some group, such as former political prisoners. Often, I would wonder why I was there. Then, I would have to figure out some job-creating opportunities for them. After an hour, we always settled on something each group liked, made sense, and was doable. I must say that I was very impressed with the people I met in Belfast from all sides of the conflict. They had great potential, if they could just stop all this violence and focus on competing in a global economy. My experience was that if you gave them a good idea, they would run with it and make it better.

Belfast City Hall before a dinner hosted for me by Lord Mayor Alban Maginness.

A DINNER

At left is a picture taken in the Belfast City Hall before a dinner hosted for me by Lord Mayor Alban Maginness, the first Catholic Lord Mayor of Belfast, and his wife Carmel, the Mayoress. (Note her chain of office). I am signing the guest book. What is remarkable about this photo and the evening is that there are Belfast City Councilors present representing the key parties in Belfast, including the DUP, UUP, SDLP, and the Sinn Féin. Never in their lives had they ever sat down to dinner together before this night. Jobs and economic development were the one issue they were willing to come together on, and that was what we were all about. Directly behind me is Dr. Frank Costello, who has done much to link Boston, Derry, and Belfast in joint economic initiatives. Beside him is Joe Corcoran, an old Boston friend who was in town looking at housing opportunities. I had met him on the plane coming over and invited him to the dinner.

"I would do anything to help Diddy out with any of her events but jumping out of an airplane is not one of them."

At Joe's right, behind the Mayoress, is now Sir Reg Empey and also former Lord Mayor of Belfast. Reg told me the story of how his wife had organized a big charitable event and arranged for a parachutist to jump into the event. However, the parachutist pulled out at the last minute, and she was distraught. Now her event would be ruined. The press was expecting it, etc. So, Reg told his wife, Estelle, that he would jump in his place even though he had never jumped before, and he did. I would do anything to help Diddy out with any of her events but jumping out of an airplane is not one of them. Also, I smile when I think of all the interesting places Reg could have landed in West Belfast if he got blown off course.

Belfast is an unusual place with lots of very interesting people. For example, to Frank Costello's left is Alex Maskey, City Councilor, who would become Belfast's first Sinn Féin Lord Mayor. He would go on to generate a lot of respect from all as Lord Mayor. Previously, he narrowly survived being assassinated, and he still had the bullets in him in this picture.

Meánscoil in their beautiful new facilities

ANDERSONSTOWN NEWS, Saturday 7 January 1995 - Page 3

Ironic cheers as Meánscoil is first to benefit from Europa bash

Major conference proves a Godsend to Meánscoil

Some people may have been quick to ridicule John Major's much-heralded economic conference held in the Europa last month - but not Meánscoil Feirste.

For as a direct result of the visit of some influential United States delegates to the school during their stay in Belfast, the city's only secondary level Irish language school is $10,000 better off.

The recent decision of the Department of Education to refuse grant-aid to the cash-strapped school caused widespread outrage not only in Ireland, but in the United States too. And that outrage was turned into practical help by Mr John Cullinane of the John Cullinane Corporation in Massachusetts. He made an emergency appeal to the American Ireland Fund, of which he is an executive member, for cash assistance for the school.

And that appeal is due to bear fruit next Tuesday when the money will be presented to the grateful staff of the Meánscoil.

The Cullinane Corporation is one of the largest software companies in the United States, and as a direct result of the intervention of the influential businessman - who stressed the urgency of the Meánscoil's plight - the application was processed in just a couple of weeks.

A delighted Seamus Mac Seáin, Meánscoil Director of Finance, warmly welcomed the news of U.S. intervention in the school's dispute with the British Government. "Not only does this generous donation go a long way to ensuring the school's economic viability, but it also shows just how much the school and what it stands for has impressed those hard-headed businessmen from America," he said.

"Not only is the school fulfilling an obvious need in the community, but it is doing it with imagination and verve. The academic results are second to none and the dedication of the teachers is something to behold. The children love their school so much that absenteeism is virtually unheard of. You would think the British Government would be only too anxious to assist in such a worthwhile venture, instead of doing all in its power to wreck it."

Mr Mac Seáin said that Mr Cullinane's experience at Meánscoil Feirste was not an un[illegible] one. He said that anyone who visits the school quickly understands the terrible injustice perpetrated on it and leaves with a determination to do something about it. "We know that John Cullinane is only one of a growing number of people all over the world intent on taking up the Meánscoil's case."

John Cullinane: American businessman made crucial Meánscoil intervention

MEÁNSCOIL

As I have said, I had wisely retained Frank Costello to help me while on the Weld Trade Mission. He scheduled me all day, every day. In the process, there would be some unusual stops. One was to an Irish language school in West Belfast called Meánscoil. I was reluctant to go because I was in Belfast about jobs, not schools. However, Frank was persistent, so I went along with my son, John, Jr. It was located in a very old church building full of eighty bright young faces in their classic school uniforms. Also, its graduates were doing very well in competitive school tests. In speaking with the Headmaster, it was obvious that they were desperate for money. They were just holding on by a thread, but what could I do about it? Then we went on to our next meeting.

"Now Coláiste Feirste (Meánscoil) is housed in a first-class facility with seven hundred students in West Belfast, with many of its graduates being a force for good in Northern Ireland."

However, when I got back to Boston, I thought about all those bright young faces and decided to send the school some money through The Ireland Fund, and that is all there would be to it. I did not know that sending this money would set an unanticipated result in motion. That is because my donation, added to The Ireland Fund, got a lot of publicity in West Belfast. In the opinion of Frank Costello, all this visibility about an American businessman and The Ireland Fund supporting an Irish language school led the British government to decide to fund Irish language schools just as it did Welsh language schools. Already PM John Major had gotten very favorable publicity from it in West Belfast, of all places. (See newspaper headlines). In other words, the donation would turn out to be a godsend to PM Major as well. His staff must have been ecstatic about it.

Now Coláiste Feirste (Meánscoil) is housed in a first-class facility with seven hundred students in West Belfast, with many of its graduates being a force for good in Northern Ireland. It is still hard to believe that my donation would lead to all this.

Binational Industrial Research & Development Foundation

THE BIRD

BIRD stands for Binational Industrial Research & Development Foundation. It made Israel the power it is today in venture capital and high tech. The United States put up $50 million, and it was matched by the Israelis. The income from this fund was used to encourage Israeli companies to engage in joint ventures with American companies, a very good idea for a small country. I thought this would be a good idea for Northern Ireland. The Commerce Department of the Clinton Administration bought into it, particularly Virginia Manuel and Chuck Meissner. Unfortunately Chuck would be killed in a plane crash in Bosnia with Commerce Secretary Ron Brown.

"A further complication was that no one I met knew anything about the BIRD except President Clinton. Frank Costello was a big help in all this as he often knew the staff members."

However, President Clinton would announce RADIUS, as it was called, on his first trip to Belfast. Also, it would be the first cross-community economic initiative in the history of the island of Ireland as a combined group went to Israel to learn how it worked. The Israelis were very helpful. The head of BIRD at the time even visited Northern Ireland. I also met with Ed Mlavsky, a former American high-tech executive who took over the Israeli BIRD when it was floundering and made it so successful. He also was very helpful and supportive. A chip design company that was a spinout of Queens University is an example of how it worked. It had designed advanced chips to handle video, very important at the time. An American chip manufacturer was very interested in it. The BIRD equivalent in Northern Ireland, RADIUS, funded a joint venture between the two companies to prove the technology would work, and it did. The Belfast chip company was on its way. I tried to get the Republic of Ireland to implement an Irish BIRD, but I could never quite get them to do it. Still seems like a great opportunity to me.

INDEPENDENT INTERNATIONAL COMMISSION ON DECOMMISSIONING

General John de Chastelain

Brigadier Tauno Nieminen — Andrew D. Sens

Dublin Office
Dublin Castle
Block M, Ship Street
DUBLIN 2

Tel No: (01) 4780111
Fax No: (01) 4780600

Belfast Office
Rosepark House
Upper Newtownards Road
BELFAST BT4 3NX

Tel No (028) 90 488600
Fax No: (028) 90 488601

23 March 2000

Mr Francis Costello
Costello Associates
3 Hampton manor Drive
Belfast BT7 3EN

Dear Mr. Costello,

Thank you for your letter and for sending us Mr John Cullinane's proposal of a Virtual Arms Bank for putting arms "beyond use"

The members of the Commission have studied this proposal carefully. As it departs from the methods approved by the two governments, and includes a time-frame that extends beyond that included in the Good Friday Agreement, we have forwarded copies of it to the two governments for their information and consideration.

We are grateful to you and Mr. Cullinane for making this helpful suggestion available to us, and we will ensure you are advised if we are able to make use of it

Thank you again for your interest and consideration.

Sincerely,

John de Chastelain

Hosting an event for Gerry Adams on his first visit to Boston, per request of Senator Edward Kennedy (l-r) Vicki Kennedy, John Cullinane, Gerry Adams, Diddy Cullinane, and Senator Edward Kennedy.

Frank Costello received this letter from General John de Chastelain.

GERRY ADAMS

Frank Costello arranged for me to meet with Gerry Adams in a storefront in West Belfast. A couple of very tough-looking bodyguards flanked Gerry. I swear I heard a shot fired outside, but nobody blinked. I made a mental note not to sit with my back to a window next time. I remember telling Gerry where my parents were from in Ireland and saying that just because my mother only went to the eighth grade did not mean she was not smart. This seemed to resonate with him. He liked us because he said so in Gaelic to an aide, and Frank overheard him. Afterward, he came to an event that I was participating in regarding jobs for Belfast and left me a personal note. This was significant because the IRA had a history of blowing up jobs. Maybe, change was in the air?

Later, when Gerry Adams was granted a Visa to the United States, Ted Kennedy asked me to host an event for him. It was held at the Park Plaza Hotel in Boston. The audience was Irish American, all right, but different from the Irish Americans at The Ireland Fund dinners. They were more working-class like my relatives, who were all from Ireland.

At one point, the peace process was hung up on decommissioning of IRA arms. Hard to get one side to give up their arms when the other side does not have to. I had an idea of a "Virtual Arms Bank" that could work and forwarded it to Frank Costello. He, in turn, delivered it to General John de Chastelain, who oversaw decommissioning, and to others with close ties to the IRA. There seemed to be considerable interest in it on both sides.

As a result, I met with those with close ties to the IRA, and Gerry Adams, to explain it. This was an interesting experience with lots of unusual security present. A chip could be put in each weapon or cache such that if anyone disturbed them, it would be known right away. I happened to know a company that had the technology to monitor these chips via satellite. However, before we got too far with the idea, the arms situation was resolved by burying them in cement. However, my sense is that there was considerable interest in it on both sides.

Pat Hume, Mark Durkin, John Lewis, and John Hume walking the Derry Peace Bridge

CITY TO CITY

Diddy had done much with her Black & White Boston efforts to bring Black entrepreneurs together with the White corporate power structure in the City of Boston when it just was not happening. It was rare when White Bostonians had any interaction with Black Bostonians in a social context, such as a golf tournament. I would be a beneficiary of this effort as I would get to know and become friends with many Black people in the city and learn what they thought. Many are still friends to this day.

Eventually, Boston would have a City-to-City program that visited Belfast that I was part of. Easily, 50% of the participants on the trip were of color, such as Reverend Ray Hammond and his daughter. Being from Boston, the participants were incredibly surprised to find that Martin Luther King, Jr., was a hero in Irish Catholic West Belfast. Murals of him were on walls in their neighborhoods as a role model for peaceful protest. Such a march, led by John Hume in Derry, would explode into Bloody Sunday and the "Troubles" for thirty years. Incidentally, as much as John was interested in political justice, he was incredibly interested in jobs. He knew their importance. As he often said, "You can't eat the flag."

"Being from Boston, the participants were incredibly surprised to find that Martin Luther King, Jr., was a hero in Irish Catholic West Belfast"

However, one participant of color on the trip said that she had never seen such discrimination as she had witnessed in Northern Ireland. Yet, everyone looked the same. They were all White. They even had the same names, albeit with slightly different spellings. In other words, for the first time in her life, she learned that color has little to do with discrimination. It has everything to do with who has all the political power, the economic power, and good jobs that go with them. The Catholics had none of these in Northern Ireland. Ironically, the poor Protestants did not have much more. You end up with the poor fighting the poor over what is left.

John Cullinane speaking at graduation day via Zoom.

Some of the first class of Onwards and Upwards receiving their OCNs.

ONWARDS & UPWARDS

Frank Costello wanted to help young people in Northern Ireland, both Catholics and Protestants, up the economic ladder, particularly those that dropped out at an early age. Some are as young as 14-16. So, he put together a program called "Onwards & Upwards." Each week a group of students that he recruited gathered in a community center in South Belfast for training in coding. They are taught and mentored by a group of very senior and experienced professionals. This includes creating a proper CV and cover letter, plus access to a real job.

The first group has now graduated with their OCNs, Northern Ireland's education authority's certificate for occupational training in basic coding outside the classroom. These young people have accomplished something very important. As a result, they now have a resume.

"Any young people that Frank and his associates can get in that door makes for a very successful program and helps the peace process in Northern Ireland."

It is the Northeastern Co-operative model, which was so helpful to me. Education combined with a job. I know firsthand that opening that first door is the hard part. That is what Frank is helping them do. Once in that first door, it is possible to open all the other doors. As Frank can tell you, kids at this age respond greatly when someone shows interest in them. Otherwise, they can get into trouble. Any young people that Frank and his associates can get in that door makes for a very successful program and helps the peace process in Northern Ireland. That is why I have been pleased to be able to support his efforts and work with him on it. It is very cost-effective. Frank is very well suited to the task because he has incredible social capital in both the Protestant and Catholic communities in Northern Ireland. He is unique in this regard. He also has a Ph.D. in Irish history which helps him understand both sides. Pictured at left is some of the first graduating class with their OCNs. The next step is a job.

Diddy and me on first skiing trip with good friend Paul Doherty who would go on to Chair the English Department at Boston College. He thought the "Jasper" story was very good, high praise indeed.

Skiing Black Mountain in Maine.

CHAPTER 11 | PERSONAL

THE SKIER

Diddy liked to ski, so we went with a ski club to Black Mountain in Maine with good friends Paul and Billy Doherty (no relation). Since I had never skied before, I was banished to the beginners' slope with the little kids. This was a drag. However, I quickly realized that skis were just long skates, and I knew how to skate. I just had to learn how to stop with them. After a while, I got the hang of it, and I was on my way to the top of Black Mountain, not a formidable mountain, I might add. I skied down with no problem. The other skiers were amazed that I could go to the top in one day and kept saying it all evening. I felt a little sheepish because what I had accomplished was stopping rather than skiing. However, this praise was nice to hear, but a little athletic accomplishment has always made me a little on the cocky side, something of a character flaw.

The next day we went to Mt. Cranmore and its famous skimobile ski lift, now gone. We took the skimobile up to the first exit point, where I quickly noticed that they had what I call a "girl catcher." This was an interesting job that the attendant seemed to enjoy very much. The girls seemed to enjoy it, too. The skimobile would just slow down enough so the passengers could jump off holding their skis and poles, but, so encumbered, stopping was a challenge. The girl catcher was positioned to catch skiers so that they would not run off the platform. He caught only girls I noticed. But this is just an aside because one member of the group wanted to go to the top, which we finally agreed to do.

In the lodge at the top, I met a girl I knew from Arthur D. Little, Inc. She asked, "How long have you been skiing?" I said, "Since yesterday." She was impressed, but I think a little skeptical. Finally, we asked someone which was the easiest trail down, and they pointed the way. When we got to the trail, it was not a trail at all. It was a cliff, and no one had skied down it yet. It would be a terrifying experience as we tried to get down. Knowing how to stop did not work on this cliff. There was no stopping. We kept falling and rolling down. At one point, I was buried in snow when I heard this cheery voice from down below call out, "Hi, Jack." It was my friend from the lodge whizzing by on the right trail. I wondered, "How did she know it was me buried in all this snow?" Also, it was a perfect comeuppance for my cockiness.

Peabo Gardner

Arthur Chisholm

Northland Pro, Neutral, 7 lie— Note no curve on stick. Teams lost Stanley Cups, Beanpots, etc., because a player couldn't lift a puck into an open net on his backhand or shot over an open net because of the curved stick.

HOCKEY WITH BOBBY ORR

A member of a country club that I belonged to asked me if I wanted to play hockey with the club team that Sunday, which was a first. When I said OK, he asked if I could get Bobby Orr to play. Bobby was on my company's Board of Directors at the time. I do not know why, but I said I would ask him, even though this was a very unusual request. What was I thinking? Bobby, surprisingly, said yes. I did not mention this to anyone, just in case he didn't show up. Also, if the word got around that he was playing, the result would be a huge crowd. Amazingly, he did show up.

After warmups, everyone threw their sticks in the middle of the ice (this is how the teams were chosen), and then we went to our respective benches. I was sitting next to Bobby when a player came late and was waved to our team. His name was

"When he saw Bobby for the first time. I could see his eyes behind his wire face mask become wide with amazement."

Peabo Gardner and his son, incidentally, was the seventh generation of Gardners to play hockey for Harvard. Peabo climbed over the boards and sat down in an empty spot next to Bobby. I could see Peabo's eyes behind his face mask begin to look to the left to see who was on his team, a natural thing to do. Then, he turned to his right. That is when he saw Bobby for the first time. I could see his eyes behind his wire face mask become wide with amazement. "Bobby, what are you doing here?" he exclaimed. Just seeing Peabo's expression made the whole experience priceless and lasting.

Bobby Orr made a perfect pass to me on a breakaway during the game. I missed the net. I was furious. I knew I would never get another chance, and I didn't. It was that miserable curved stick I had to use. They do not make sticks anymore like the one that Arthur Chisholm, Northeastern hockey legend and high school friend, gave me many years ago. It almost resurrected my hockey career, along with a pair of old skates from Billy Fahey that fit perfectly. It was a Northland Pro, Neutral, 7 lie, a veritable scoring machine because, among other things, you could backhand a deadly shot with it.

Bob Bland (right), with his wife Judy, receiving commendation letter in Turkey.

WORST FLIGHT

The weather was terrible, so I decided to skip the 7:00 am Eastern flight home to Boston from Washington, D.C., and wait for the 9:00 am Northeast flight. Shortly after takeoff, the pilot informed us that a plane was blocking the instrument landing runway at Logan. However, he said it would be cleared away by the time we got there. This did not happen despite his optimism along the way. As the hours dragged by and we flew in dense fog, I thought I was in an episode of *The Twilight Zone.*

Everybody has terrible flights. However, what is unusual about this story is that many years later, I was playing golf with a very good friend, Bob Bland, and we were comparing our worst flights. Bob told me about an experience he had with an equally miserable flight from Washington, D.C., to Boston. His plane lost its nose gear while landing in a snowstorm at Logan. No one was hurt, but the pilot asked Bob, who was in his Navy uniform, to help him get everyone off the plane by encouraging them to slide down an escape chute. However, they all had to wait for a bus in the sleet and snow. Then we realized that it was his plane that prevented my plane from landing. If I had taken the earlier flight, as I intended, I would have been on the flight with him. It might have been a much easier flight or, at least, shorter.

In recent years, Bob has been heavily involved in creating the Wyss Institute at Harvard, which focuses on biologically inspired engineering. It is funded by his good friend, Hansjörg Wyss, with some of the largest personal gifts in Harvard history. The Wyss Institute encourages research ideas across multiple disciplines that will not only lead to the solution of major problems but also the creation of new companies with all the skill sets necessary to bring them to the marketplace and capitalize on them. It's a very sophisticated, well-financed, imaginative undertaking with a lot of potential.

Bob, and his wife Judy, in turn, established a very imaginative and well-endowed "Emergency Fund" in their name at Wheaton College to help students, as Judy was, in times of emergencies, so that they, too, can stay in school.

Professor Raymond Robinson, everybody's greatest teacher.

THE GREATEST TEACHER

I grew up in the middle of history in Arlington, Massachusetts. Massachusetts Avenue was lined with reminders of those days. Every April 19, Paul Revere and his aide Dawes would stop at the Arlington Town Hall on their way to Lexington and Concord, and the shot would be heard round the world. I even worked in the Jason Russell House, where the British massacred all the people in the cellar in their frantic rush to get back to Boston.

Yet, I remember my classes in History and Government as being incredibly dull despite all this history being right outside our door.

It was a remarkable history, as a rag-tag bunch of farmers and tradesmen routed the mighty British Army. This had never been done before. We never discussed these monuments, or the people named on them, or visited "the rude bridge that

"He soon brought history and government to life. It became an incredibly important and exciting subject, which democracy is. I was witnessing, for the first time, the impact of a great teacher."

arched the flood." It was like it was ancient history. I visited the bridge for the first time a couple of years ago and noticed that just as you got to it, there was a stone commemorating five British soldiers buried there. Who were they?

This was true at Northeastern University, as well. Then, Northeastern changed instructors in our class and put in Raymond Robinson. We were dubious of him at first. He was very young, not much older than us, with long, skinny fingers, horned rimmed glasses, and bookish looks. However, he soon brought history and government to life. It became an incredibly important and exciting subject, which democracy is. I was witnessing, for the first time, the impact of a great teacher, and he was a tough marker, too. It was ironic because we learned more but got lower grades. I never had the chance to express my appreciation to him until nearly fifty years later, when, ironically, I ran into him right outside Cullinane Hall. He did not know who I was, so I just pointed at the Cullinane name on the building.

President William Dill of Babson College welcomes Inductees.

INTEGRITY IN BUSINESS

When I was inducted into Babson College's Academy of Distinguished Entrepreneurs, as part of my remarks I said that integrity in business was not a liability but rather a great asset. Afterward, the President of Babson, William Dill, sought me out to tell me how much he appreciated my saying this because it was counter to what some in academia thought and taught.

This is ironic because when I started in business, I thought you had to cut corners to succeed. I decided that I would not do it that way, even if I failed. The opposite was true. I learned that doing business with integrity was not a liability but a great asset. It is pretty basic. People like to do business with people who treat them fairly

"Doing business with integrity is such a great asset. There is nothing like a great reference. Also, it is a much more pleasant way to do business."

and honestly. We never had a lawsuit with a client in the twenty years we were in business. In contrast, a fellow CEO who was the founder and president of a major computer company told me that if you do not have some lawsuits going, you are providing too much service to your clients. He had forty laws suits going at the time. To me, this was crazy. It still is.

Sometimes I would get a letter from an irate customer. I would not duck it as much as I would like to, but instead, I would call the person who sent it to me. He would be astounded that he would be receiving a call from the president of the company. After the call, I would take his problem to my person in charge of customer support, Gary Wright, for follow-up and resolution. A couple of weeks later, I would get a call from the same person, and I would groan, thinking that maybe we hadn't resolved the problem. Invariably, he was calling to thank me for solving it so expeditiously. The company now had another great reference. What else did I have to do that was more important? You can bet he talked to his peers about the experience. Also, when he moved on to a new company and was in a position to buy a database management system, you could be sure he was very likely going to buy ours. That is one reason why doing business with integrity is such a great asset. There is nothing like a great reference. Also, it is a much more pleasant way to do business, and employees like it.

Uncle Walter Fitzgerald, on the left, and his friends John Fleming and Thomas Quinlan from Dunmore East, County Waterford.

British ship, the SS Laurentic

LAYING A WREATH

My uncle, Walter Fitzgerald, lost his life in WW1 when his British ship, the SS Laurentic, hit a German mine coming out of Lough Swilly in County Donegal off Northern Ireland. It was January 17, 1918, and the ship sank with 357 souls lost, many by freezing. My mother had his medals from the British government, and they always fascinated me. The ship, built at Harland and Wolff shipyards in Belfast, home of the Titanic, was bound for Canada carrying 3,200 bars of gold, worth $50 million at the time. Divers would recover all but eight bars.

When I was at Letterkenny Institute, some people secured a boat to take me out to lay flowers over the ship, but I winced at how small the boat was. Fortunately, it

"Irish Catholics serving in the British Navy and sailing on a ship made by Protestants in Belfast at Harland and Wolff Shipyard. Now people know who they are."

was a lovely day with calm seas because the North Atlantic looked like it could be a very formidable place. When we got over to the SS Laurentic to lay the flowers, the captain showed me the ship on the sonar. I had not expected this. The outline of the ship was right there below us. It made for a very emotional experience as I dropped the flowers over it. The captain told me that his grandfather heard the explosion when the ship hit the German mine.

There is a monument to them in Buncrana on Lough Swilley where the survivors were taken and many who lost their lives were buried. Not far away, ironically, is a monument to Tip O'Neill, whose family was from the area. There was a song of the time, "Pack Up Your Troubles," that my mother disliked intensely because it reminded her of the loss of her brother.

I think it is very good to bring people back from the dust bins of history if you can. For example, my uncle's picture and his friends from Dunmore East, County Waterford, who died with him, were featured in an *Irish News* story. These were Irish Catholics serving in the British Navy and sailing on a ship made by Protestants in Belfast at Harland and Wolff Shipyard. Now people know who they are.

This is exactly how the students looked when we visited the first inner-city school we made state of the art in internet technology.

E-RATE

I accidentally overheard a Dean of a local business school say that the Catholic school kids were behind the public school kids in computer technology. I mentioned this to Peter Lynch, and he asked me to chair a committee to improve computer technology in the inner-city schools of the Archdiocese of Boston.

Our first committee meeting was at the school Superintendent's office in Dorchester. Present at the meeting with her were other Nuns and some school administrators. The school buildings were about 100 years old. The wiring was so bad that teachers could not have a light on and heat coffee simultaneously. This was hopeless.

I said as much to the group. I thought there was no way that they could become state of the art in Internet technology. One young man interrupted and said, "We've done it," he was from the poorest school in the City of Boston, Cathedral High School. I asked him, "How did they do it?" He said, "E-Rate." I said, "What's E-Rate?" He explained that it was money provided by the government based on taxes on cable companies. It was administered by a subsidiary of the FCC and paid for Internet services, routers, cabling, etc., in schools. However, the schools had to get volunteers to wire the schools, run cable, find the computers and software, etc. The poorest schools got the money first based on the school lunch program. So, I said that if Cathedral could do it, the other schools could, too, and we would undertake an entrepreneurial effort to do it, but below the radar. The Catholic schools had not been taking advantage of E-Rate. Incidentally, E-Rate was something that then-Congressman Ed Markey promoted.

First, I visited Mayor Menino to see if he would allow us to use his E-Rate consultants because the City of Boston had tapped into E-Rate big time. He agreed even though the schools are competitors, and this help was very important. Within six months of our first meeting, we had the first inner-city school state of the art in Internet technology as part of a $3.5 million E-Rate grant with the great help of Don McInnis, a former DEC Senior VP. It was impressive to see these kids gathered around big-screen PCs with instantaneous responses, donated by companies such as Fidelity and EMC. Parents and other volunteers had wired and cabled the schools to make it possible. The teachers, too, were thrilled with all the attention.

Great White Shark

THE GREAT WHITE SHARK

Since the movie "Jaws," many people have been terrified of sharks, particularly Great White Sharks. Great White Sharks have been passing Chatham, Massachusetts, for probably thousands of years as they swim worldwide. However, much has been made of Great White Sharks around Chatham in recent years.

My interaction with a Great White Shark came when I was slowly cruising around in my 26-foot Grady White Fisherman, exploring an inlet called Fools Cut south of Chatham. I noticed something dark behind my engines. I thought it was seagrass at first, but there was no seagrass there. It was all sandy bottom. Besides, the dark

"It was right under my boat in eleven feet of water, and I could see it. I could touch it with a pole if I wanted to, but who would like to do that?"

something moved with me as the boat moved. I sensed right away what it was. It had to be a Great White Shark. Soon it was right under my boat in eleven feet of water, and I could see it. I could touch it with a pole if I wanted to, but who would like to do that? Its nose was just beyond the center console, and its tail was beyond the engines. This meant it had to be at least thirteen feet long. We cruised along this way for a while.

Then, it headed south toward the tip of Monomoy, and I headed north toward Chatham Harbor. I had not bothered it, and it had not bothered me. Many experts say that the sharks are after the seals, and they certainly are in other parts of the world. From what I can tell off Chatham, they kill very few, though. Maybe, if they find an injured one, they kill it because I know from first-hand experience that seals are incredibly fast and elusive. I suspect sharks are smart enough to prefer munching on dead whales to chasing very fast and maneuverable seals unless they have to.

Of course, if you want to attract a Great White Shark, just jump in the water where they might be and splash around. They will think you are a seal in trouble, and they will be very interested. A Great White Shark tagging group proved this on a very hot day off Chatham. They jumped in the water and were splashing around. The spotter in the plane above them radioed them to get out of the water and fast because some sharks were headed their way for some reverse tagging.

"There's no friends like the old friends."
James Joyce

OLD FRIENDS

Billy Fahey was my oldest friend, smart, witty, and he and his wife Kay were beloved by all. As the years passed I got to appreciate Billy more and more. He was also the town historian. He seemed to know everyone. With Billy it was never about him. It was always about the other person. When he died, he had so much recent tragedy in his family that he left word, no wake or church service except for immediate family. The only service was at the cemetery, and his name wasn't even in the obituaries. That was Billy. So few knew of his passing, yet the cemetery was full of people. One would think the Mayor of Burlington had died.

Paul Welch and Bob Keating were two of the funniest people I have ever met. Hanging around with Paul Welch was like spending time with Jonathan Winters. Also, he and Bob were great putdown artists. When I brought Diddy home to meet them and others I knew for the first time, did they say, "What a beautiful girl. Where did you find her?" like regular friends would? No, their observation was that she was the first good-looking girl that I ever had a date with. Not true, but it makes me laugh every time I think of it. Of course, then there was great friend Billy "Emma" Doherty who delighted in catching you in some foible with a wicked sense of humor.

Billy Fahey with Paul Welch and Bob Keating, two incredibly funny people at an unusual serious moment.

Hazel's Bakery and the origin of the Malcom Butler cookies.

MALCOLM BUTLER COOKIES

Hazel's Bakery is a family-run bakery in Needham, Massachusetts, which I go to all the time. The people who run it, Stacey and her husband, Steve, and all their employees are very nice. It is a throwback to a family-owned and run business. They know their customers and will even make up a personalized birthday cake for you on the spot. They often bake cookies with a theme, such as sports, when some big game is in the offing, like the Super Bowl.

The year the Patriots lost the Super Bowl because Bill Belichick did not play Malcolm Butler was an unusual example. Patriots fans thought this was a horrendous decision at the time and very un-Belichick. It was right up there with Grady Little, Manager of the Red Sox, not taking Pedro Martinez out and losing the World Series.

"Incredibly, the Patriots recently re-signed Butler with a two-year contract, but there were no Malcolm Butler cookies to be had at Hazel's the next day."

I thought people would forget, and it would blow over. However, when I went to Hazel's the next morning, I noticed that they had baked Malcolm Butler cookies. It made me smile. Wow! That is how upset people were that Belichick did not play Butler. Hazel's was baking Malcolm Butler cookies as a result! It sure was not blowing over.

So, I emailed Dan Shaughnessy, *Boston Globe* sports columnist, about it. I thought it was something he might find interesting. He responded and asked if he could use it on the radio program that he would participate in that morning because it would be all about Bill's decision. I said sure, why not, and he did. A Boston TV station noted his comments and had a television truck and crew out at Hazel's filming it all afternoon, including the cookies. Hazel's had become famous, and their phones were ringing off the hook by people looking for those "Malcolm Butler" cookies. The next day when I went to Hazel's, they were all excited by the experience and wondered how it happened.

Incredibly, the Patriots recently re-signed Butler with a two-year contract, but there were no Malcolm Butler cookies to be had at Hazel's the next day. I do not know why, but that is just how it works. Malcolm did not make the cut this time.

Boston Red Sox Impossible Dream team of 1967

Wayne Turner holding the Beanpot Trophy. At right, Coach Fernie Flaman and Mrs Flaman—Northeastern University hockey team Beanpot Tournament winner in 1980.

Raising the banner

THE IMPOSSIBLE DREAMS

The Red Sox taught us that we would always lose the big game. First, they lost the 1946 World Series to the St. Louis Cardinals in the seventh game on a controversial play. Then things did not go well in 1947. Then in 1948, they lost the Pennant in a playoff game with the Cleveland Indians. This was brutal because the manager, Joe McCarthy, pitched Denny Galehouse, a journeyman, versus his all-star, Mel Parnell. The game was over before it had hardly begun. We were crushed. Again, in 1949 the Red Sox lost the Pennant on the last game of the year to the New York Yankees in a very controversial way. It was just as brutal. Then the hoped-for "Glory Days" were suddenly over, and the doldrums set in for almost twenty years. There was no hope anymore.

Then came the "Impossible Dream" of 1967. The song was adopted as the theme, and it was so fitting. No Red Sox fan had ever experienced anything like this. It captivated the City. They won the Pennant. No one cared whether the Red Sox won the World Series or not. That would be asking too much, but still, they almost did. The Red Sox had done in the curse of losing the big games.

However, the Red Sox was not the only impossible dream. Over at Northeastern University, its hockey team had not won a Beanpot Tournament in twenty-five agonizing years. In fact, they had never won one, ever. Then, in 1980, as the game remained close, everyone in the Boston Garden sensed that, maybe, this might be the year when it was going to happen, and it did in overtime. The winning goal was scored by Wayne Turner, perhaps the only Black player in all of Division 1 college hockey. The crowd went wild. Everybody in the old Boston Garden was rooting for them, even fans from the other teams. One of my key VPs from the company, Bill Casey, came to the game with me. He was an avid photographer and, amazingly, caught some of the key goals which I was able to forward to players such as John Montgomery. There's nothing better in sports than to finally win something when you have been beaten down forever, an impossible dream.

Joseph E. Aoun, President of Northeastern University.

Joseph Aoun, Northeastern's incredibly successful President, attended his first hockey game the night they raised good friend Billy "Emma" Doherty's jersey, a former Captain, to the rafters.

Dot and Larry Broderick

George Caner, Jr.

Bill Deery and John Cullinane

THE GREATEST GENERATION

I was a small boy when the Japanese bombed Pearl Harbor on a "Day of Infamy." All the older boys and girls in the neighborhood went off to war. Amazingly, two crew members that flew in Jimmy Doolittle's famous "30 seconds over Tokyo" squadron were from Arlington, Howard Sessler and Gene McGurl.

I would get to know three of "The Greatest Generation" besides my brother-in-law Bill Eidson and cousins. They were Larry Broderick, Bill Deery, best of friends, and George Caner. Incidentally, they would scoff at that Greatest Generation tag. Larry Broderick originally was in a ski battalion but switched to the OSS, the forerunner of the CIA. Tragically, all his friends in the ski battalion would get killed in a railroad

"I would get to know three of 'The Greatest Generation' besides my brother-in-law Bill Eidson and cousins. They were Larry Broderick, Bill Deery, best of friends, and George Caner."

tunnel in Italy when the Germans fired a cannon down it. Larry would spend two years behind the Japanese lines in Burma and narrowly escape being captured. When taken out by a small plane for R&R once a month, he would go to the resort featured in "The Bridge On the River Kwai." Bill Deery was on an LSD off Okinawa as a decoy ship for Kamikazes. His ship would be hit, and he would get wounded while the Captain and five others were killed. He told me that he could see the plane coming, but he could not get the gunners' attention because they had just shot down another one and were celebrating. Bill could be so calm that he once slept through a typhoon while at sea. This made for a great golf partner.

George Caner, another friend, fought all across Europe as a point man for his artillery unit. Point men usually lasted about thirty seconds, but he survived for two years, got a Bronze Star, etc. Never mentioned it, though. He was a historian and wrote a paper that said we were very lucky to win in Europe. The Germans were very good at war.

The Group

Gerard and Marilyn Doherty

Dr. Heinz and Johanna Schonmetzler

Thalia and Dr. Nick Zervas

George and Gail White

Ann and Brian Caputo

THE GROUP

Each event that Diddy and I were involved in would require that we put together a table of ten guests or more for the dinner. It required a lot of work because we wanted to make sure everyone was compatible and would have a good time. However, we were involved in so many events that this became very time-consuming. Eventually, Diddy said, "Why don't we just invite the same people each time instead?" That is what we did. However, while they were all our friends, our guests were strangers to each other. Yet, they would all become great friends for life. They included George and Gail White. I first met George when he

> *"Our friends, our guests were strangers to each other. Yet, they would all become great friends for life."*

hired me as a sales trainee at CEIR. Then there was Gerard and Marilyn Doherty. I met Gerard at the JFK Library Foundation. In addition, there was Dr. Heinz and Johanna Schonmetzler. Diddy met Johanna while playing tennis in Westwood. Then there was Brian and Ann Caputo. I met Brian when he sat beside me at the Northeastern University Freshman orientation at Symphony Hall, we were friends ever since. Rounding out the group was Dr. Nick and Thalia Zervas. I met Dr. Zervas via the Dukakis political campaigns and at Longwood Cricket Club. We certainly participated in some great events as a group.

Bill Sahlman, Professor of Business Administration at Harvard Business School.

BILL SAHLMAN

Bill Sahlman is a Professor of Business Administration at Harvard Business School. I first met Bill, along with Howard Stevenson, as a Northeastern entrepreneur when they were promoting entrepreneurship at the HBS when it seemed like a poor relation.

Bill believes in these companies succeeding but also doing good. He has shown the way by directing a lot of the focus of the HBS on medical problems. For example, as head of development, he used the massive fundraising power of the HBS to help create the very important Harvard Stem Cell Institute. Once, he called me when Ted Kennedy got sick with glioblastoma to say an Israeli startup company he was involved with called Novocure had technology designed to curb it but, unfortunately, it was too late. The company now has an $8 billion valuation, so it must have something that works for anyone stricken with it.

"What I find fascinating about Bill is that he is always into something different and significant. For example, he is now involved in a company founded by a 99-year-old scientist"

However, what I find fascinating about Bill is that he is always into something different and significant. For example, he is now involved in a company founded by a 99-year-old scientist, Dieter Gruen, who has remarkable credentials, including escaping from Nazi Germany. Dieter has been awarded six patents in the solar cell space since 2010 and has helped form a company called Graphene Solar Technology to exploit them. They can produce cheap, rugged cells manufactured in the US and four times as efficient as current cells. This means they can be used in many other applications. It is very important stuff.

Not long ago, I met Ivan Sutherland, the "Father of Computer Graphics." Everything in computer graphics is based on his Sketchpad that he created at MIT Lincoln Labs many years ago. Now he is at Portland State University, inventing asynchronous chips with his wife, Marly Roncken. They believe such chips are the way of the future if we are to remain competitive in computer technology. Very timely given the chip bill just passed by Congress.

I know what Bill is up to. He is sending a message that talented people like this can still make major contributions to our society regardless of age. I find this very inspiring.

CHAPTER 12 | ADDENDUM

HUMOR

I thought I would end with a little humor. There seems to be very little humor today, so I thought I would include a few stories that made me laugh. Some of them are black Irish humor, which the Irish are particularly good at. For example:

The Explosion

Two little old ladies are in their apartment in West Belfast when they hear a big explosion. One says, "Oh my God, Jesus, Mary, and Joseph, what was that?" The other said, "Oh, it was just a bomb." The other says, "Thank God! I thought it was thunder and lightning."

The Yamaha Motorcycle

A young man in a small town in Ireland got a new Yamaha motorcycle. He was trying it out when he saw his good friend on the road. He invited his friend to go for a ride, but his friend declined. The zipper on his jacket was broken, and it was a cold, raw day. The driver said, just put it on backwards, and everything will be fine, so he did, and off they went. After a while, the driver looked back, and his friend was gone, to his horror. He must have fallen off. So, he retraced his route and saw his friend lying on the road surrounded by a group of farmers. When he got there, he asked the farmers, "Is he Ok?" One farmer replied, "Yes, he seemed ok, only his head was turned the wrong way. When we turned it the right way around, he has been quiet since."

The Chocolate Chip Cookies

There was this 100-year-old man on his death bed in Ireland. He did not have long to go. Then, he smelled chocolate chip cookies being baked down in the kitchen by his wife. There was nothing in this world that he liked better than chocolate chip cookies. So, with great effort, he dragged himself out of bed, got himself down the stairs, and dragged himself into the kitchen. Finally, he was able to get to the table where the cookies were cooling. When he reached up for one, his wife took the wooden spoon and rapped him on the knuckles. "Away with ye now," she said, "We're saving those for the wake."

The Bonus

Tim and Bridget came from the Old Country. Poor Tim. He never learned how to do anything. He never learned how to read or write, but he did learn to drink. Finally, someone got him a job down at the pier as a longshoreman. Sure enough, didn't he get drunk and fall off the pier and drown. At the wake, Tim's wife Bridget was sitting with her friend Deirdre. Deirdre was a little thing with her shawl around her but very sharp-eyed. She never missed a thing. Well, the head of the longshoreman's union came over to Bridget and said that they had collected $5,000 for her. Bridget said, "Oh my God, Jesus, Mary, and Joseph, $5,000! Poor Tim and me never had two nickels to rub together, and now $5,000. Poor Tim, he never learned how to do anything; he never learned how to read or write." Deirdre leaned over and whispered in her ear, "It's a good thing he never learned how to swim."

EPILOGUE

Everyone has lots of stories that would be interesting to others. I think they should write them down and include pictures whenever possible. Writing this was fun. The stories just flowed out. In my case, I was up to 160 in no time, and I think of more all the time, some crazy, some I cannot even tell. Then, when looking for pictures I found some great ones I never saw before. I cut the book back to one hundred or so stories. I do not consider it an autobiography. Maybe, it's more like the "Canterbury Tales," although not as bawdy as the one I read.

It is helpful to see the irony in things, though. Things are rarely as they appear to

Things are rarely as they appear to be to the outsider, and weird things happen all the time.

be to the outsider, and weird things happen all the time. For example, one can be a big shot in Las Vegas on Sunday night with your name on The Great White Way, and then on Thursday night be at the airport, hungry, with no restaurants open, and nobody knows your name or cares. That is what this book is all about.

My company made much of it possible because Diddy and I were often drawn into things such as co-chairing events. At the time, husbands and wives just did not do this. None of it at the time seemed like a big deal but, looking back, it was and it is still going on.

Others have different and unusual stories to tell that I would like to read. They can tell their own Canterbury Tales.

Diddy and John (Photo courtesy of Boston Symphony Orchestra)

AUTHOR'S BIO

JOHN CULLINANE

John Cullinane founded Cullinane Corporation, the first successful software products company in the computer industry. Ironically, at the time, industry gurus said there was no future in software and that it could not be done. Others had tried and failed, predicting that he would, too. However, the great success of his company would prove to Wall Street and the computer industry that a great deal of money could be made from treating software as a product. Many software companies followed, and an industry was born.

John was invited to be the first President of the John F. Kennedy Library Foundation. After seven years in this role, he became Chair of the Foundation's International Visiting Dignitaries Series that welcomed many world leaders to the Library, including Nelson Mandela on his first visit to America.

John has been the recipient of many awards and honorary degrees, including the first Honorary Degree ever awarded outside the island of Ireland by the University of Ulster for his work in helping the peace process in Northern Ireland through jobs. This ceremony took place at the JFK Library, as was the Irishman of the Year Award from the Friends of the JFK Library. He was also inducted into the Babson College Academy of Distinguished Entrepreneurs and the Infomart Information Processing Hall of Fame. In addition, he was the first Fellow in the Center for Business & Government at the Kennedy School, Harvard University. As a social entrepreneur, he created the Boston Public Library Foundation and was the Founder of The Friends of Belfast. He also was a member of the Aspen Institute's Middle East Strategy Group.

John is a graduate of Northeastern University and recipient of an Honorary Degree. He is married to Diddy Cullinane and they have two children and four grandchildren.